UNSPOKEN
AGREEMENTS

UNSPOKEN
AGREEMENTS

A Journey towards
your Inner Light

AKK

PARTRIDGE

To order additional copies of this book, contact
Partridge India
000 800 10062 62
orders.india@partridgepublishing.com

www.partridgepublishing.com/india

I dedicate this book to the teachers of my Life,
My mom(KK), My Gurus, "Sai Baba" and "Sadhguru".
They have helped me grow by letting me know, that
learning is never ending, so learn and just flow.

Today is my thirty-second birthday. More than anything, I am gripped with fear and anxiety. Just a few days back, I had received some horrible news about my left ear. For the past few days, my left ear had been acting up, and I had seen few doctors. They had examined and given me some weird diagnosis about the same. Finally, I decided to visit the best ENT specialist in town. I was hoping for a clear diagnosis. Well, after checking and posting a few scary questions about my ear, he finally concluded that I was suffering from a Sensoryneural disorder, which has basically affected my hearing in the left ear; and apparently, there was no clear treatment for the same except for steroids and hyperbaric oxygen treatment. That, too, is with very slick odds of working. In fact, as per him, even hearing aid would not be of much help to me as the nerve itself had gone dead, so I was pretty much looking at a possibility of a permanent hearing loss without anything for me to be able to do about it.

This was the time when my best friend was living with me for more than six months now. She had left her house in other city due to some conflict and I was happy to support her through this transition. Just recently she had managed to find her accommodation and had moved out of my house. We had been friends for more than six years, but over past few days, things were a little rough between us. We were not talking much, but when this news hit me, all I could think of was talking to her and sharing my worry. But despite all my efforts to contact her, she seemed determined not to talk to me. Finally, I mustered courage to message her,

> *'Hey, hope you are fine. I really want to talk to you. There is something I want to tell you, something related to my health. Well, I saw an ENT specialist today, and he told me that I am at a risk of permanent hearing loss in my left ear.*
> *Feeling very scared.'*

Back came a response. And I anxiously and desperately reached out to my phone to read the message. I was shocked to my core to read the reply,

> *'Well, you deserve it as you are not used to listening to anybody.'*

For a second, I couldn't believe what I was reading. My eyes filled with tears, and I was convinced that she must be really upset with me. Otherwise, this kind of response was impossible to come from her, as she was one of the kindest people I had ever known. And that's when it hit me. That I may have caused her more hurt than I knew. I now am wondering whatever conflict we have had in those past few days were not that grave to cause this kind of rift between us; and though my primary worry was regarding my hearing, I couldn't get my mind off to what can have the power to terminate a relationship, or any relationship for that matter.

As I continued thinking about, it I realized that my pain of disappointment also emerged from the breach of an expectation 'unspoken agreement' I had with my friend, which is 'When I need you, I expect you to be with me irrespective of the conflict we are dealing with.'; and as I kept victimizing myself that how could she not fulfill my expectation, doesn't she know that to be a good friend you need to be forgiving when it is of medical emergency, and then another counter thought came to my mind, 'that, 'Is there a possibility that she may not know about the expectation I have from her', because the fact is we never spoke about this, I just assumed that she has to know this as I know, Simple! Hence, it dawned upon me that this is it! The assumption I am making right now is what is creating so much of pain for me and maybe I too have failed to fulfill one of her unspoken expectation, which may have turned her against me. So that's when I finally realized that this kind of 'unspoken agreements' we all have with each other can cause the strongest of relationships to break. As these agreements may become bigger than the emotions or intentions we have for each other. We end up giving so much of power to these agreements we hold even without our awareness.

As I kept ruminating over these thoughts for a few days, I soon realized that I may have a tendency to hold this Unspoken Agreement where I expect the other person in any of my relationship to always be at their 'best'. Then that may mean as per me is best understanding, lots of patience, ability to forgive and help, fulfill most of my expectations if not all as I would expect and most important Love me under any circumstance.

It didn't take me long to understand that I have approached this in a completely wrong way. I can decide for myself how I need to be and not burden other person with my expectations.

CHAPTER 1

Exploring Self

'I will be the better half in every relationship.'

As I hear this statement, a lot of questions arise in my mind. Also, a sense of resistance that when there are always two or more than two people in a relationship, why should I, alone, attempt to be the better half? Does that mean that I will be like a push over that everybody can take advantage of?

The answer is no. The idea is to not feel powerless, but to empower yourself by taking responsibility, which is— as rightly said—the ability to respond. We cannot change anything in our life until we are ready to take responsibility for it. Most of us misconstrue responsibility as being blamed for. But the true meaning of responsibility is to be able to understand the situation at hand, and be ready to do something about it. Either make it better, or have the courage to admit that it cannot be changed and move away from it. It's the idea that, after all, our first relationship is with our self and even here, 'I will be the better half'. Situations in life or relationship may never be perfect or the way you wanted but your response to them can definitely be the way you want

As an advanced race, we need to focus on improving the quality of our life rather than just enhancing our standard of living. These are two very different things. It's redundant to accumulate money by compromising our health and peace of mind to eventually use it all to pay our medical bills to heal our bodies.

We have all the comfort and luxury possible, but we still live in stress and desperation most of the time—not to mention the insecurity we feel in everything we do. In the pursuit of proving ourselves powerful, we end up killing each other. We may have evolved enough to live in cities, but still follow jungle rule where the whole existence is around pleasure and survival.

Now, before we start talking about relationship, let's talk about who we are. A question been asked for ages now, and lot of attempts were made to answer this. Here is my understanding about this.

The self is nothing but the 'Holy Trinity'—the body, the mind, and the soul. Having said this, deep inside the vaults of our consciousness, we know that we are still beyond this! For example, how can we explain phenomenon like intuition or emotional sensory perception or even past life regressions?

The Holy Trinity or the beyond—what is self? Which one of these, or any other theories, is right? This is a question, which does not have a definite answer. Each one of us can choose to have our own answer, and all of it is right! We are who we believe we are. There are a lot of philosophies, as well as scientific explanations, attempting to help us understand our reality. But the interesting thing is more we understand about us, there is more left for us to know, or to explore, as we all are super dynamic beings.

Here lets explore one of the aspect of us, the mind. Thoughts emerge from mind and these thoughts are what lead to emotions. For example, as we wake up in the morning, as we realize its Sunday we feel relaxed but similarly a Monday morning can bring emotions of resistance, tiredness or sheer exhaustion even without starting to work. This way, we can experience the connection between thoughts and emotions. So it's our thoughts about a certain individual or an event or an experience that determines our emotion about it. What's more important is that we have the power to choose the thought that makes us feel peaceful. But the problem is that we are reckless thinkers. We get one thought, and we go on attaching one thought after another to it; hence, we attach strong emotions to that string of thoughts. This snowballs into everything we think and feel about in our life. These thoughts play a vital role in relationships too.

Now lets move to the other aspect which is body, I think we all can relate to this part very well as we all have lots of tangible evidences to prove to us that we are physical beings, in fact we just don't believe in it but live our entire life preserving, protecting, and indulging in all kinds of experiences which would give us physical pleasure and comfort. Sometimes even the aim of life just revolves around our physical existence. At this point some may argue that we have this experience of life because of our physical existence, but if we are just supposed to eat, live and die then why are we born as human beings and what is the difference between us and the animals who exist around us, what is in us which makes us different from them except for our ability to think. Having said that the composition of our body is so amazing that with proper training and discipline it can do amazing things including Self-healing, by just changing the way we sit or by focusing on our breath we can entirely shift our energy levels. The body is also more capable then we might know, as there is an entire science called Kinesiology which studies body movements and the response of our body in every life situation, also there is something called as muscle-testing in Kinesiology which can help us determine what is good for us, or also determine truth. These modalities work with the concept, *"Body doesn't lie"*.

The most interesting aspect, that I would like to discuss here, is the soul; it can be regarded as the element, which gives life to the body. For most of us that which is not a part of our physical experience doesn't exist but the funny part of the soul is that you cannot experience it through physical means, you can only experience this if you learn to go beyond your body or senses or once you are dead or even in deep meditation. Mind and body both have a sense of Identity but what goes beyond the identity is the soul.

Lets understand this in a better way through the use of an analogy of a person who bought a new house, the house can be considered as the Body, the contents of the house like the windows, the porch, the ceilings, the balconies and so on can be regarded as the Mind, while the person who is going through the whole experience can be reckoned to be the Soul.

In this book we primarily will be talking about thoughts/mind as its important to start with an aspect we are able to relate to the most when we are about to embark on a journey of Self-Discovery.

Coming to the mind part of us and the thoughts, which are created. Most of the relationships break due to baseless assumptions and careless generalizations that are generated in mind, where, in fact, every complaint we have about another person in any relationship is merely a reflection of our own inner state. The other person is like a mirror. Whatever is inside of you is easily projected on the other person. Yes, it's true. As unsettling as it may be, every external experience we partake in is based on what we are willing to see or explore within ourselves. For instance, I used to always complain about how it drives me crazy when people don't keep their time commitments only to realise that it a real challenge for me to keep my time commitment with anybody, and all my attempts to change that have horribly failed. Also when we condemn a certain behavior of a person, our brain cannot differentiate between the person and the behavior, because of that we may end up hating the person exhibiting that behavior. What we have failed to understand is that this behavior is just a part of the other person and not the person. Well, as mentioned above most of the times even condemning any behavior may be wake-up call for us to reflect and see what we are supposed to learn out of it.

CHAPTER 2

What are Unspoken Agreements??

'The mental suffering you create is always some form of non-acceptance, some form of unconscious resistance to what is. On the level of thought, the resistance is some form of judgement. The intensity of the suffering depends on the degree of resistance to the present moment.'

– Eckhart Tolle

Lets define Unspoken Agreements: They are those thought arrangements that are formed between us and other people, circumstances, or ideas that generate a certain kind of advantage for us. These agreements may have the power to justify our feelings, thoughts, or actions. As rational beings, it's quite likely that we create these agreements to prove ourselves right, save ourselves of any guilt for feeling negative about other person or situation, or to even conceal our emotions. Our true nature is joy, and at the very core of our being, we all understand this fact. So every time we feel anything other than joy or peace, we need to explain to ourselves that it's justified for us to feel away from joy or peace at that moment. That's how unspoken agreements (UA) emerge.

We thus use UA to conceal our true emotions, and feel 'reasonable' to be feeling discomfort—the discomfort of being anything other than joy and peace. All human relationships are need-based relationships, and we *use* each other to fulfill these needs. Yet, the true essence of a relationship can only be felt when we learn to go beyond our needs. In relationships, we don't want anybody to fix us. All we desire is just total acceptance, understanding us without being critical and judgmental, which is true for each one of us. As per me, the biggest unspoken agreement in relationships we deal with is that either you can love the other person, or you can love yourself.

The true reason why the relationship was created is to experience intimacy and oneness. Though we always attempt to establish our individuality and mostly vouch for stand alone culture, the matter of fact is from the point of our birth to where we are today we have reached with the contribution of other people in some way or other. We all somewhere do believe that we work well when we are in a team.

The most intimate relationship is a romantic relationship and the relationship between a mother and a child, as in these two relationships; we get an opportunity to exercise extreme oneness. The sense of separation seems to disappear, and we feel and think of the other person as of our own self. When we actually demonstrate oneness, then—and only then—we experience the true joy, as we are our true self.

Relationships are nothing but reflectors, and all the people who come in our life teach us something about our own self. It's a kind of a reflection of relationship that we have with our own self. Most of the times when we feel hurt, pain, or disappointment in a relationship, it's always due to some 'lack' we experience in our own self, and relationships kind of give us the feeling that the lack has been taken care of. But the real challenge is to know that it's not the other person fulfilling this lack, but us doing it for ourselves through them. Even if worst possible things happen in a relationship, it's not going to take anything real away from us unless we want it! By real, it means our ability to be happy or to love or to forgive, as these are the true essence of our being that nobody or nothing can rob us of.

Continuing here the exploration of ourselves as discussed in the previous chapter, there is a scientific study in quantum physics which says we are energy beings. This energy field, long been known to healers and mystics, is now verified by scientists. Everything in the universe consists of vibrational energy including our physical body. Quantum physics has shown that matter is simply a certain vibratory rate of energy. Matter and energy are two different manifestations of the same primary energetic substance, of which everything in the universe is composed, including our physical and subtle bodies. The vibratory rate of this universal energy determines the density of its expression as matter. Matter, which vibrates at a very slow frequency, is referred to as physical matter. Our body is made of cells; these cells are made of molecules, which are made of atoms. Atoms are made of subatomic particles. These subatomic particles are not made of energy; they *are* energy!

We and everything else are one big mass of energy. Spirit and mind puts together, this energy has been put into the physical shape that you see with your limited senses. Thus, matter is energy. Remember Einstein's equation, $E=MC^2$? It means that any piece of mass (M) is energy that can be calculated by multiplying this mass by the speed of light squared. We are literally made up of light; we are energy beings.

Thus, this is our true nature; and all the laws, which govern energy, are applicable to us, as we are energy. This implies that we attract like energy, keep ever expanding, and are ever evolving. Since the attraction is so strong for the like energy, separation causes pain, as it needs us to go against our true nature. Experiencing and demonstrating this oneness gives us real pleasure.

Some may debate, at this point, that some of us do get pleasure in hurting others or causing pain. It's very important to be able to differentiate between real pleasure and derived pleasure. Real pleasure is directly realised, and once realised, it becomes our second nature. It originates from within us, and is up to us to experience whenever and wherever we want to experience it. On the other hand, derived pleasure comes from outside, and we need to keep on working to gain it. For example, we feel pleasure when we buy a new car. We feel happy about it, drive it, and then carry on with other aspects of our life as usual. When we meet with other challenges, the pleasure derived from buying a car is somewhere lost as we get on with dealing with other challenges of life. So derived pleasure fades away, and this is not the real joy or pleasure I'm talking about.

As we generally hear people say, we're all wearing our pair of glasses, tinted with colors of belief, values, and our sense of right and wrong. We see the world and relationship through these glasses—rose-tinted, black and white, and murky brown, or what we have on.

Our brain is a very interesting and obedient organ. If we believe that something is negative, it will give us enough evidences to believe so; and if we believe that something is positive, our brain will again prove it to us that whatever we are thinking or feeling is right. So it's not just entirely our brain that creates thoughts, it's us and the personal choice we make in every moment, is what decides our perception towards something.

For Example: The reason we place so much importance on our first experiences, like our first kiss, our first day at work, etc. is because we are fully present in the moment and thus enjoy it to its fullest. However, eventually, we get used to the experience and decide in our heads already what the experience is going to be like. This way, we deprive ourselves from the magic, the uniqueness that such experiences can provide us.

Let us learn to be in the Moment

Most of the saints and great thinkers say that 'Only the present moment is real'. I struggled to understand this for a long time, wondering what it really means. And finally, one day while talking to my friend, I realised what it means. I won't get into the painful details of it. However, let me take you through my journey as a participant in that sharing, and as she was talking about her past, and sharing all the sordid details with so much of accuracy that it felt as if she is going through the whole experience right now in this moment. With her description of the situation, I could not only visualise how the event must have occurred, but also feel the emotions of all those who were involved in that situation she described. The pain, the anxiety, the voices, the expressions, and everything that could make it as real as it was for her in that past event.

That's when I realised that past is gone, and so are the happenings along with it. However, She managed to keep it alive and fresh, reminding herself of every single emotion she felt along with it and relived the whole experience once again.

This means that we don't just remember the event, but also all the emotions we felt at that time when it occurred. And every time we recollect that incident, our brain unconsciously helps us remember every single thing we felt, sometimes we may also add some more emotions while recollecting the event hence making the experience very intense and real for us.

Now, if by any process or means I can change the emotion of that experience, my whole version of the story would change. The best part about this thought is that I can do this consciously in this very moment, and so can you! That's why I always say, '*This moment is very powerful.*' That means if you want to make amends its now, if you want to learn something its now, if you want to express something its now, if you want to heal yourself its now and if you want to achieve something, once again its now.

By living in the moment, you can bring about any change you desire, and thereby change your whole reality, as I had also mentioned earlier the importance of being in the moment.

Experience is nothing but occurrence of one event after another, moment after moment. Every moment choose to act from a space of love and compassion. First of all, start doing it for yourself, as we cannot love or accept others unless we totally love and accept ourselves. Without self-love (here, I mean a healthy state of self-acceptance with which comes healthy appreciation of everything and everyone too and not in a sense of vanity), the effort to love someone or do something for someone is futile. This incomplete effort will not yield anything. as this half hearted attempt may give you a temporary sense of happiness that you were able to be of some help to other, but if the response is not as you expected it to be then you may in return end up feeling more resentful and victimized.

Although it is ideal to be in the moment, more times than not, we are either stuck in our past or anxious about our future; and without dealing with these two aspects of our life's timeline, it's difficult to be fully present in the moment.

Lets see how we can deal with the pain of our past by making use of our present moment. Pick up any event of your past, which may be causing pain, anger, regret, or any other unresourceful emotion. Use a blank paper to assess the event with more clarity. To begin with, remember to choose an event that is emotionally less intense, just till we can get the hang of the process.

1. Identify every character of the event. Don't leave out a single person that you associate with that particular event.

2. Now recognise every (negative) emotion attached with every person and make a note of it on the paper.

3. Next, change the emotion to a positive emotion. Such as, if the negative emotion was 'angry', then one of the positive emotions that you can replace it with can be 'patient' or 'accepting'. If you find this difficult, then at least change it to an extent where you feel neutral about the person. Just remember this: *There is always a positive intention behind every behavior.*

4. As you change every emotion attached with every person, notice your state of emotions.

5. Next, forgive every individual including you. (Further we will also learn more about 'Forgiveness', which can make this exercise easy)

6. Acknowledge and appreciate the event, and thank it for all the wisdom it brought in your life.

Next lets see how to deal with the anxiety of the future using the power of present moment. Identify what you want to manifest in your future and are feeling anxious about the same. Let's focus on one goal at one time.

I.

To bring in clarity of what you want, make a list of reasons why it's important for you to manifest this certain goal, note down at least thirty reasons for now. As you will start doing this, you will realise how important it is for you to manifest this. Please note one of the main reason there is a delay in manifestation is because we keep on changing our minds regarding what we want, as every time we make a wish, universe is set on a course to bring it into our reality; and as we keep changing our mind about the same, hence, a new course is set causing the delay, so it's very crucial to be absolutely clear about what you want and have a steady mind about it. Sometimes, there will be obstacles in the way, but it's very critical that we stay focused and keep on wishing for the same thing. Also, necessary actions in that direction is also required.

II.

As you recognise the goal, declare the goal to at least five people as a self-induced pressure on self to keep the commitment toward what you want to achieve.

Once the goal is recognised, let's do a future visualization and see yourself to have already achieved it.

1. See the things you would see once you have achieved the goal. Make a note of every single detail as possible.
2. See a very realistic situation, which you find easy to believe.
3. Now, feel the emotion you would feel as your wish is being manifested. As you identify this emotion, increase the intensity of it and feel your whole body being one with this emotion.
4. See your eyes, then your face, and see your whole body. Now, hear the words of your future 'you' telling your present 'you' the words like 'great job', 'you are almost there', 'you are on the right track'. There will be moments of doubt/fear, just acknowledge them and immediately get rid of them as they have no business bothering you. Universe has already granted you your wish; now, its just matter of time before you experience it in your reality. Start believing this and acting like you have already got what you wanted.

III.

The most important step after the visualisation of the goal achievement is to completely forget about it and continue taking appropriate steps, which would help in the manifestation of the goal and refrain from getting obsessed with the result., Here is a small poem with the help of which I am trying to catch the essence of the above concept.

"Let past be gone,
And the future has still not dawned
But the present is where you belong
So live life like a song, which would rhyme
With every aspect, that is forth drawn."

Once we learn to live in the moment, lets understand how to create a fulfilling life experience.

Life is not an assessment, but merriment! We have a right to enjoy the riches of life, and all the aspects of our personality that make us who we are. We don't need to suffer for any higher good, and everything in life can be experienced with ease and peace. How do we do this? All we need to do is to learn to live every moment being in alignment with our highest true joy—joy like giving, loving, forgiving, caring, accepting—and stop obsessing just about our individual survival and our individual requirements.

Our highest joy cannot be in anything that somebody else needs to do for us like 'I feel joy when somebody loves me' or 'I feel good when somebody cares for me or appreciates me'. That is not joy; that is our ego feeling good, which feeds on somebody else doing something for us. It may satiate us momentarily, but not make us feel joy. True joy lies within. We identify every relationship from ego standpoint. This way, we feel pain if our expectations are not fulfilled or somebody does not act as per our wish. All this pain that we engage in experiencing emerges from ego.

We live our lives based on the memories we have created, and use our past as a reference book for ourselves. When, in relationship, you start asking 'WHAT ABOUT ME??' more than often, it's time to think about how much you're giving into the relationship. For all you know, it may turn out that it's *you* who isn't giving 100 per cent in the relationship! In any kind of life decision, make yourself—and only yourself—100 per cent responsible for your happiness. Remember that people and external situations cannot be held responsible for what belongs to you—your happiness. This awareness brings us to a space of unconditional 'givingness', and frees us of any expectations or disappointments that may meet us otherwise. More than anything else, this frame of mind helps us enjoy the process called as Life entirely.

Also relationships are created for completion of our experiences, and every relationship is pure because we give one part of us in every relationship. The most important relationship in human life is considered to be the romantic relationship, since in this relationship—in its complete form—we experience the maximum extent of physical and emotional oneness with the other person. All our life, this desire of being one with another person drives us. In this form of a relationship, we experience the true bliss—the bliss of oneness. Due to this kind of intimacy and identification with the other person the possibility of maximum unspoken agreements is most likely in romantic relationships than compared to others. Now lets gain some more understanding about the Unspoken Agreements.

Unspoken agreement (UA) is nothing but the perceptions we create for our own security and most of the UA we start creating from our childhood by noticing our surroundings, maybe also by the behavior of people around us and through our early life experiences.

This is done in an attempt to avoid pain, and thus shield us from fear of the unknown. Our need to feel secure is dire thus we get along with people who share the same UA as ours. As we are an integral part of the nature we too crave to live in harmony and peace like other living beings, but being trapped in the illusion of separation we end up making each other's lives difficult. Wherein we have the maximum potential to love and to offer. Yet, we end up forgetting our true potential of maintaining harmony and balance.

Based on prior experience, or preconceived notions, sometimes, we foolishly believe for certain things to be in a certain way and expect the other party involved to know it too without verbally expressing what we have in mind! Mind is the reservoir of all the thoughts, beliefs, values, and the impressions created from the time of our birth (or probably even before that). The mind maybe a creator of thoughts but as mentioned before as well that we are the ones who put attention on things we want to hence creating our own version of reality which most of the times maynot even be the truth. So we should learn to understand the truth then being stuck with our own belief. That's why it's said,

> *"You don't believe things because they make your life better, you believe them because they're true."*

> – Veronica Roth, Allegiant

The language of the mind is emotions. Most of us feel that we have no control over how we feel, and that thoughts just 'happen' to us. The interesting thing is that just by putting our attention on our emotion, we cannot only understand how and why we feel the particular emotion, but that we also have the power to change the emotion. Just by monitoring our emotions, we can actually distinctively understand our thoughts., and also consciously change them as well.

We Can Choose How We Feel

Why is it important to know so many things about emotions.?As emotions can play a very important role in self-intervention. Most of the resolution takes place through self-intervention. We will discuss more about emotions in further chapters. Before we continue lets understand some more things about self as now we realize that we are not just a thought creating machine or a perfect system of all the bodily organs, but so much more that that. Here are some interesting observations about self (us)

The biggest breakthrough in the path of self-intervention is '*to know that it's okay to be wrong*'. For most of us in our growing years, we have always been corrected and always been told how we should be 'correct' and it's almost a crime to be wrong. Unfortunately, we still carry those impressions in our minds, which influence our way of thinking and the way of seeing the world around us!

'Most of our relationships fail because of our need to be right.'

We are attached to our version of truth, which is why we face resistance to change it. That's because we haven't just believed it to be true, but also lived on basis of that version of our truth. As mentioned before thought creates emotion, emotion creates experience; experience creates belief, that eventually creates our reality;. Paradoxically, everything emerges from a thought, and to change all of it, (the belief, the emotion, the experience, and our version of reality), all that needs to be done is to alter our thought that creates all this. So our belief is nothing but a culmination of our experiences, which defines our reality.

Ultimately we need to understand that though thoughts create emotions, by consciously choosing the right kind of thought we can create emotion which is conducive with the reality we wish to experience.

For example: As a child if I have only heard stories of how difficult it is to earn money and how hard you must work to get it, also that its never easily available, then my emotion about money is going to be fear based and my belief would also be very negative which eventually even in my grown up years is going to reflect in my experience with money. But if with the help of some self-work I consciously am able to change my thoughts about money then definitely my experience would also change.

The next observation is that in a relationship or any other aspect of life, as the going gets slightly tough, we want to quit what's going on as it seems like an easy alternative. It's so easy for our ego to choose a path of least resistance whereas, in fact, great growth and learning comes from walking on the path we are most uncomfortable with or outside of our comfort zone, as stretching our limits cannot just help us overcome our fears, but also enhance our confidence and sense of freedom.

One of the most important step in overcoming our fears is to refrain from extreme thoughts such as quitting, divorce, suicide, or any other extreme form of avoidance, as it becomes the way of thinking—perhaps a habit, which can create a lot of stress.

For example, any car owner would know that for a smooth functioning of a vehicle, it's always suggested that we maintain a steady speed. This enables the building of mileage and durability of the engine. Can the vehicle touch top speed or the slowest speed? Of course, yet for good maintenance, it's not recommended. Just as erratic speed patterns can ruin the vehicle's overall performance, an extreme thought can really affect your overall well-being and make you fearful.

Also understand that every time you are stressed, the secretion of certain hormones, like oxytocin, increases extravagantly. This is because the intention of the body is to protect itself through this emotional turmoil. If we keep stressing ourselves out constantly, eventually, the immunity system of the body fails. That's when we fall extremely sick. Despite the existing suffering, if we still continue the same stress pattern, it's quite possible that we may attract some chronic diseases our way, and eventually death. While this whole process may be excruciatingly painful physically, it is even more painful emotionally and mentally. So the right way of maintaining the balance within, as well as outside, is to be thoughtful, aware, and to learn to pause rather than merely being a puppet to our emotions and situations.

But why would we adopt such a behaviour if it is so harmful to our complete well-being? Well, our subconscious is very smart. One of the purpose of this part of brain is to get the desired result; another is to protect us. So in any tense situation, the mind helps us put the behaviour, which would fulfill either one of these two purposes. And we will see further how our subconscious is still influenced by our primal instincts.

Subconscious is like a 5-year-old child. A 5-year-old will know when to cry, when to be cute, and when to throw tantrums to get what she/he wants. In conflict-like situations, our logical mind shuts off and subconscious takes over. It then makes us put on behaviours like yelling, crying, or having thoughts like quitting.

Any such behaviours, which can give us a quick recovery or a short-term solution, can actually be disastrous in the long term. So every behaviour, no matter how negative, is adopted because we see an advantage in adopting it. With this happening repeatedly to give us our preferred advantage, it becomes a pattern, which we eventually come to identify as a habit. By the time something becomes a habit, we would have convinced ourselves that we have lost our ability to control it consciously.

Exercise:

How to maintain a healthy state of mind:

1. Pause
2. Name the emotion
3. Observe the emotion
4. Control the need to speak
5. Listen, rather than hear; don't listen to merely reply. Notice how much of whatever is being said by you, or the other person is actually true. **If what you hear is true then you don't have a right to react and if it's not true then you don't need to react**

CHAPTER 3

Reasons for creating Unspoken Agreements

The first reason can be: "To Be Resistant to Being Wrong"

The resourceful state of mind is the one where there is no obsession to be right. Rather, it's a space where we are okay with everything and anything around us. In this state, we tend to avoid having strong opinions; we're ready to be challenged and altered. It's a fact that true growth happens only then. I personally call it developing 'Okayness' which is being okay even when everything around you doesn't seem to be okay. As this state can help you find solutions even in the most dire situations.

A wise person once said, 'When you speak, you are just repeating information you know. But when you listen, you may end up learning something new.'

We can benefit in our personal growth, as well as in relationships, provided if we have an open mind and not stuck with what we think we know including our beliefs, opinions, as well as our perspective. Even the greatest minds on the face of earth believe that they don't know everything, and there is always something more they seek to learn, and that is the reason why they reach the heights of greatness in their respective fields. Great minds are aware that the human brain's function is limited to absorbing, analysing, understanding, recreating, and representing information. Although a brilliant gift of nature, its work heavily relies on input of information. And that can happen only if we are open to ideas and new learning. So most of the great learning happens when we have the courage to say 'I don't know' as a lot of possibilities can arise from here than when we say 'I know'. As the scope of something new comin up is just nipped in the bud.

Apart from the above reasons, there are a few more reasons that can drive us to create UA.

Identification (With-in)

Many a times, we suffer because we identify too much with what is going around us, and with the roles that we assign ourselves, like being a good professional, a good father, a good partner, and so on. Not only do we identify ourselves with our roles and the circumstances we are in, but also keep assessing ourselves on how we perform in these roles and circumstances.

The game of acquiring/possessing, as humans from a very young age, we understand that we cannot enjoy something fully or be able to control it to our satisfaction unless we possess it. For example, if as a child we liked a particular toy, which doesn't belong to us, we kind of stay fixated on that toy and kept longing for that more than the other toys; hence, this idea gets implanted somewhere in our minds of how we have to possess/acquire something to be able to enjoy that and also make it belong to us. The caveat here is that this identification may be fruitful to a large extent for materialistic gains; however, when this extends to our relationships, it can be quite a different story.

For example, in a marriage, or even a romantic relationship, one often says to the other that you are mine; hence, as we believe it to be so, all the idea we have about what is it like to be when something is mine gets associated with the person, even before we realise we start obsessing over how to keep him/her mine. The need to identify with something (an experience, a status, or a relationship) is the need of the ego. It emerges from a fear. Love has no such needs and neither does love demands this kind of possession.

Another example of this may be a high ranking official retiring from his job after a long service. Being so used to the respect and honour, which comes along with the post, he lost his sense of respect and esteem, also his sense of identity.

These kinds of identifications can cause a lot of trouble in the experience of life itself. In relationships, this can influence us to want to control the other person, which in turn may not be appreciated/accepted, since we as a species like to experience life with a sense of freedom and not captivity of another person's expectations (which emerge from false identification).

Separation (With-out)

I personally feel separation is the biggest illusion (everybody is a stranger just until u get to know them), which has been created, and we have not only accepted it but are living it in every sense! Though, at lots of instances in life, this illusion loses its hold. Eventually, we do manage to slip back into it, mostly at times when we start living life surrounded by question, 'What about me?' or 'What's in it for me?'

This is the fundamental question of the business world, and we sometimes use it even in our personal life. If you find yourself doing this in your personal life as well, here is what you may want to consider—you may be assuming that everything is on a transaction basis. In no way am I saying that it should mean that we just keep giving and not receiving. I'm only saying that the giving should not be depended on how much you receive. Understand that there is nothing the other person or the external situation can give us, which we can't give to ourselves; be it love, respect, peace, happiness, or anything else that you truly desire to experience. So if you choose to give, let the giving happen from the space of abundance and not scarcity. Give with no expectations, as there is nothing that you can't give to yourself, and there is also nothing that you actually need anyone to give you.

Conclusion: Though times have changed and we live a very modern and sophisticated life, we still are letting the rudimentary rules of survival influence us and how we live.

These rules also drives us to create UA's, so that we would feel safe and secure.

Some of these laws are:

1. ***Attack or be attacked***: In our life, generally the instances of being physically attacked are rare. Of course there are exceptions, but otherwise, as mentioned, the chances of the kind of attacks are scarce even though there are a lot of situations where we feel emotionally or mentally attacked. As this happens, our instinct to give back or retaliate kicks in without that being the best alternative of response at that point of time.

2. ***Belong to a group or perish***: A group or a set of people with common ideas or background provides a feeling of security, or sometimes, just approval of what we believe; and to belong to such a group can also, up to a certain extent, take care of our fear of being lonely.

3. ***Accumulation of resources is wise***: This thought emerges from a space of scarcity and fear again; thus, hoarding can give a false sense of abundance and make us feel safe. Even having a big family or lot of children can sometimes solve the same purpose.

4. ***Never rest or trust***: This philosophy, again, is for us to warn us about the impending danger, as we all live in a world of enemies; and deep down, believe that everybody around is just waiting to get you.

So always be on alert and save yourself from fear of unknown.

5. ***Be power-driven***: One who has power will most likely not face challenges in the sense of survival; and in today's world, getting power means owning a lot of money or professionally holding a big position. From here emerges the philosophy that you should always be one step ahead of others.

6. ***Life, pleasure, or survival***: And finally, all of our life experiences are either around gaining sensory pleasure or in securing ourselves and whatever we feel belongs to us.

After going through the above reasons we may be tempted to say that these are the qualities of EGO; thus my ego has to be blamed for my behavior, but the real empowerment lies in taking responsibility for yourself and every response you evoke.

Nevertheless EGO is not your enemy; for all we know it can be regarded as more of like a temporary friend. The reason I am saying this is because all the happiness we feel through our physical senses is due to our EGO but what we do in return is that we mistakenly think that this is the only way we can seek happiness, thus conveniently forgetting the temporary nature of our experience. EGO's job is to give a firsthand experience of how it is to feel all these emotions so that eventually when we encounter the real experience we may have some background. So blaming EGO is not going to help us in any

way as we have our free will to choose in every moment of our life what we want for ourselves—temporary sensory pleasure or everlasting bliss.

Some More Reasons for Creating UA:

Early conditioning: This could mean that what we have experienced, maybe with family or friends, accepted their ideas/thoughts, and adopted them as ours without much of a resistance. For example, a child watching his father insult or abuse his mother may regard that as a normal behaviour.

Environment: the culture or the community you belong to, their ideologies, perceptions regarding people, and the way of dealing with them. For example, every culture has a certain set of beliefs on grounds of religion, and people belonging to this certain group may end up accepting all the ideas and living life as per them.

Any traumatic experience: Some shocking incident or event may also play an important role in influencing these agreements. Like for example, somebody who has been cheated or deceived in a relationship may create agreements in order to save themselves of any similar experience in the coming future.

So-called universal beliefs: For instance, the beliefs around marriage and the expectations of how one should behave when married are kind of taken to be granted.

Our own internal projections on others: When we are born, the whole focus of living is to survive. Once we learn how to survive, the next step ensues—exploring the world around us, to process the information, and then to put it to good use. Next comes the step of reaching out to people. This is actually nothing, but an attempt to know our own self by knowing others. For example, what we like about people is actually what we appreciate about ourselves too! What we don't like so much about others . . . well, I'm sure you can fill in the blanks. Thus, the next step is of expressing this in every possible way. And then comes the step of gaining awareness, as in if you feel the need to criticise somebody about their behaviour, reflect within to see what is driving that need. Also, is it really about the other person or something related to you? This kind of self-reflection can help you in gaining peace and acceptance within yourself. Finally, it's about being at the state of absolute bliss. You can also call it the state of complete acceptance.

Now, as we have understood about what are unspoken agreements and what influences them in our life, let's see some life instances on how they can affect us and our relationships.

The most important thing to remember about these following stories is not to create any judgment of right or wrong, its just to highlight how we create Unspoken Agreements in any relationships we deal with.

CHAPTER 4

Unspoken Agreement in Romantic Relationship

'Our work is not to find love, but to destroy
our personal barriers against it.'

– Rumi

In most of the romantic
relationship, as we begin, its just about togetherness,
companionship getting to know each other, and learning
to love new things about each other. But as the relationship
graduates, we want to take it to other level, or getting it to
some hypothetical finishing line and the whole focus shifts
from each other and comes down to taking it to the other
level. And we able to do that or not, somehow determines
the success or failure of a relationship; and based on this

categorisation, we also decide whether we are a 'success' or a 'failure'.

Following are three stories to give us a brief idea of how unspoken agreements are formed, how they affect, and how they influence our thinking.

Story 1

Two people, Ronnie and Mary, both have had their struggles in life. Ronnie comes from a family where his parents abandoned him, and left him with some relatives to be taken care off. He grew up craving for parental love. He was ill-treated and made to work really hard from a very young age. The only thing, which helped him survive, was an image of a partner in his head. He would imagine being with her, and daily struggles did not seem that taxing. Every time he would be criticised or scolded, he would think about her and feel good about himself. Hence, days passed, and finally he left the house and got busy with developing his career.

On the other hand, Mary comes from a family where there was lot of love, sharing, caring, acceptance, and joy. She grew up treated like a princess. Apart from some or other incidents here and there, her life was pretty smooth sailing. So one day, by chance, Ronnie and Mary meet each other. Ronnie, for the first time, feels so happy. He is finally able to give face to the picture he had imagined in his head, and Mary also feels a strange attraction toward Ronnie, which she finds difficult to explain. Eventually, they confess to each other how they feel, and their affair starts.

Initially, everything is very blissful. They find it difficult to stay away from each other, thus, spending a lot of time together. Everything is really beautiful and surreal, so much so that they want more of it, and they finally decide to move in together in an apartment. Few days passed by in moving and setting up the house. Even then, things are pretty smooth, though there are some disagreements regarding the furniture of the house, but they are able to get through it.

As the closeness start growing, Ronnie starts feeling a little bit of discomfort regarding Mary's clothes, but he still keeps mum about it until there is an episode where some guys pass some lewd comments about her clothes and Ronnie loses it. He confronts Mary about it; Mary is confused and annoyed that why, all of a sudden, he is reacting in this manner. Ronnie says that he is not comfortable with the way she dresses (UA: if you love me, you should take care of whatI feel comfortable with); and Mary is not able to understand why, out of nowhere, he seems to have an issue about her clothing (UA: if you love me, you need to accept me the way I am).

The biggest UA in a love relationship is if u love me the way I want, then I will love you; hence, Ronnie and Mary fight for the first time. In any kind of conflict, it first starts in a person's mind, and then extends into a conversation. Any negative impression or thought is like a spell. You cannot fully revoke its effects even if you want to. It will always prevail in a subtle manner in the mind of both the parties involved.

Story 2

The next story is about Ben and Lily. Ben works with a big multinational company, and has a very strict policy of three dates one person whereas Lily has had a past of a broken engagement. Also seen her parent's divorce, and though heartbroken, is waiting for her Mr Perfect, so through online dating, these two meet. As Ben meets Lily for the first time, he feels like she is a special one and for once wants to let go of his three date rule and move on, but he starts looking forward to spend really quality time with her. She is enjoying every minute with him. They are blissfully in love and are sure about being with each other.

Since Ben is a very social kind of a guy, he has a lot of friends and likes to hang out with them quite too often. Initially, Lily seems to be okay with it, as she really wants him to be happy, but gradually starts wondering why she is not a part of this part of Ben's life. As time passes, she doesn't even feel comfortable that Ben really seems happy and it bothers her

Lily confronts Ben, and Ben is really upset, as he is not able to understand the big deal (<u>UA: we should be happy together 'always'</u>). He explains it to her just because he enjoys hanging out with his friends does not mean he does not love her (<u>UA: as we love each other, we need to respect each other's space</u>). But she doesn't seem to be convinced. All she wants to hear is he would not hang out with his friends, or he would take her along as well, but all Ben is saying is, 'If you want to hang out with your own friends, I would not have a problem with that.' And Lily feels, 'Wow, he really doesn't understand me. All I want is to be with him and for him to be with me. Why he is not able to understand such a simple thing?' (<u>UA: As two people really love each other, they don't feel the need to be with anybody else. Only when they are not entirely happy with each other, they connect with other people</u>).

Story 3

Third and the final story is of Raoul and Priya. Raoul comes from a simple middle class family with huge aspirations to change the world with all leadership qualities, real rebel in nature, thus challenging all the social bias; and hence, ends up having lot of followers. In the college, people feel pretty comfortable approaching him with their issues, especially girls, as they can't help getting charmed by his raw charisma. While Priya is pretty studious by nature, and though she has a thing for social work, she prefers to focus on her self-development, and then wants to get into helping others. Somehow, she can't help but notice Raoul and his work and gets attracted to him very instantaneously. Raoul also seems to notice Priya, and is floored by her simplicity and intelligence. As they both get together, they do some really exciting work as their passion seems to coincide.

As the relationship graduates, Priya starts getting a little hassled by the thing, which attracted her to Raoul in the first place, has started bothering her now. The ease with which people can approach him, and he always being available for others, and thus fails to give her time at lot of instances. They fail to have a personal life, now Priya expects Raoul to make some time for her (<u>UA: as you love me, I should be</u>

one of your priority, if not the only), and for Raoul, it may be (<u>UA: since we share the same passion, she will understand me better and will be okay compromising on a few things</u>).

So in above stories we saw how simply UA are created in our minds under such simple situations, so contemplate and see how you too maybe holding any UA in your respective relationships. As you go through the following stories do pause and take a few moments to do some reflection.

Possible UA in romantic relationships:

1. As we love each other, we are bound to remember all the important details about each other.
2. If you love me, you will take efforts to make me happy.
3. As you love me, you will put my needs before yours.
4. You will always make me feel special.
5. As you love me, you, too, should love/hate people/things I do.
6. If I am emotionally down, you should not go down at the same time and know how to pep me up.
7. As I love you, you should always take my interests into account.
8. As you love me, you should be my beck and call.
9. We should include each other in every important decision we make.
10. We should agree with each other over everything.
11. If you don't agree with my point of view, it means you don't love/respect me.
12. If you want me to love you, you need to keep changing as per my requirements.

13. As you love me, there is no reason for you to get affected by anything else in your life.
14. As you love me, you should be okay if I want to have sex with you.
15. If you reject me of a kiss/physical intimacy, then your love is questionable.
16. As you love me, why would you ever need your own space even from me?
17. My happiness is in your hands.
18. We make each other feel complete.
19. If we fight, then we don't love each other enough.
20. As you love me, you should be faithful to me.
21. All my romantic fantasies need to come true (it's meant to be).
22. If I have done some sacrifice for u, then u must also do the same.

CHAPTER 5

Unspoken Agreements
in Friendship

Friendship seems to be the most simple and most unconditional relationship, as the expectations are the lowest and the acceptance is more; and also devoid of caste, creed, or any other biases.

Story 1

Two friends, Ben and Fred, know each other since their college days, though their friendship emerged pretty much after college as they ended up working in the same company. Ben is more of an eccentric kind, while Fred shares the same eccentricity, but knows how to manage it well. Thus, they get really well, and end up having good time with each other.

As their friendship evolved, they started sharing lot of things with each other. Ben would end up spending all his money, while Fred, too, would enjoy, but also be aware about saving and securing his future. Ben started being in debt, and Fred would most perpetually help him out. But Ben wouldn't change his attitude toward money and would end up being in same debt situation almost every month. Now Fred had started getting a little disturbed with Ben's behaviour, as he would not have any remorse or even gratitude toward Fred (<u>UA: don't take me for granted</u>).

Ben is not even aware of Fred's feelings, as he believes in living in the moment and cannot understand why Fred is acting so aloof lately, as Ben feels he can manage his money issues even if Fred doesn't intervene (<u>UA: be my friend and not my parent</u>).

Story 2

The next story is about a nice group of housewives staying in suburbs. These women enjoy their time together in the way of get together like, lunch parties, celebration of birthday parties, movies, and picnics. This is a pretty tight group, as they have cherished long period of togetherness with each other, so they won't easily entertain any new person. Julie is the most social and would mostly take initiatives for all the events, and others would also willingly follow her lead. Now, Julie met Amanda, and there was an instant connection, as they were able to laugh and enjoy over almost everything. Although Amanda is a little shy, still, Julie convinces her to be a part of the group she belongs to.

With a lot reluctance, Amanda finally seems to agree with the proposition and meets the group on one of their lunch parties. These women also welcome her and make her feel comfortable.

Amanda, too, is now a part of the group and enjoys hanging out with this group, but because of her introvert behaviour, she doesn't focus on developing any individual connections with any of them. She is most comfortable with her friendship with Julie. As time passes, because of some reason, some kind of tiff rises between Julie and Amanda, so much so that they stop talking to each other entirely. Amanda decides that because of Julie, she knows the respective group, then it would be appropriated to be apart of the group as she is no more friends with Julie (UA: if I am not friends with you, I cannot be associated with your friends). As the whole group is no more close to Julie, they, without knowing the truth of the matter, start bad mouthing Amanda (UA: as your friend, I need to hate whom you hate).

Story 3

The next story is a story of Natalie and Penny who have been neighbours since childhood, grew up like sisters, and shared lot of beautiful moments together. Their families appreciate and enjoy this bond they share with each other, and so, post college, they are both doing great in their respective careers. Natalie loves clubbing, making new friends, and is kind of a free spirit. So is Penny, in her own way, but is restrained and calculative. They both are not reckless and respect each other's comfort zone.

So this new family moves into the neighbourhood and Matthew arrives in the neighbourhood, and also in their lives. They become very good friends with each other. Also, these girls trust Matthew and enjoy hanging out with him. One day, Natalie is late for work and is having real trouble with her car. Matthew sees this from a distance and proposes to give her a lift to her office. Natalie is not in a position to say no, as she is really late for her important presentation, so she agrees. This is the first time that Natalie and Matthew are hanging out without Penny.

Penny is with some friends and kind of notices Matthew's car. She even calls out to him but in no vain. Then she observes that he is not alone, and he is not with anybody else but Natalie. She immediately calls Natalie, but as she is preparing for presentation, she cuts the call. Penny finds all of this a little odd (<u>UA: we are supposed to hang out together</u>). Finally, Penny reaches her office just in time and finishes her presentation. After a while, she realises about Natalie's call and calls her back. By the time she calls back, hours have passed. Penny answers the call and talks about how she saw them, so Natalie shares the whole story about the flat tyre and how Matthew came to her rescue. Penny hears the whole thing and they hang up the call, but somehow, she is still not convinced about the story, so she just steps out of the house just to check on Natalie's car to find out that the tyres are fine without knowing that Natalie had her car taken to the garage and had managed the whole thing. From that day, Penny started keeping her distance from Natalie, and Natalie doesn't even knows what's the matter (<u>UA: if something is bothering her, she will definitely let me know</u>).

Unspoken Agreements in Friendship:

1. Even if I am rude to you, you need to be able to forgive me.
2. Respect and understand each other's differences.
3. If you reject my idea, you reject me.
4. There are certain boundaries in friendship, which one must never cross.
5. As my friend, you need to be there when I need you.
6. You cannot be more close to my friend/partner than me.
7. Don't take me for granted.
8. You have to trust me no matter what.
9. I don't need your approval.
10. You need to respect my time/not keep me waiting.
11. I deserve equivalent importance as your girlfriend/boyfriend.
12. You are my secret keeper.
13. You should be forgiving of me not matter how big of a mistake I may have committed.
14. There is always a line in friendship that should never be crossed.

CHAPTER 6

Unspoken Agreements
with Children/Parents

*"Lets learn to love our children for who they
are then who they can be".*

$\qquad$ Patanjali says in one of the
five steps of living a yogic/balanced life is to maintaining
non-stealing (Asteya), which also includes robbing your
child's chance to learn responsibility or independence by
doing something on his own. We keep telling our children
to be like somebody, 'Why are you not like him?' Or 'Why
can't you be more like your friend or father or uncle?' I think
what our child wants to hear from us is 'Be who you are and
I will love that'.

In all our growing years, we are told that we should
be serious about life, about career, about studies, then as

we grow up, we are asked, 'Why are u so serious? What happened?' And we do the same thing with our children.

Most of us as parents say that we give a lot of freedom to our children, but the point here is when did our children's freedom become our possession that we can give them that?

We all are born free, and our freedom belongs to us and only us, also the same case with our children

As human beings, our need to leave something behind is very strong. For most of us, this is one of the reasons we have kids, so that even after we die, we would prevail in some way through them. There are some who build monuments, so that despite their leaving the earth, they can still exist in some way, and people would remember them or keep them alive in their conversations/discussions. Sometimes, it becomes a purpose of life. We all want to be known for something, as this can give us some sense of success in life. We may end up burdening our children with this responsibility of fulfilling our incomplete dreams or of doing things that we couldn't do, but we need to keep this in mind that they have their own soul purpose and we need to respect that.

Story 1

This is a story of a couple, Lisa and Ted, who were trying for a long time to have a baby. Finally, after a lot of trips to fertility clinics and IV specialty clinics, they were successful to get pregnant. They both enjoyed every moment of the nine months right from ANC classes to dietician visits. They also put a lot of thought and creativity in decorating the nursery for the baby. Finally, the big day arrives and after six hours of labour, Steve is born completely healthy and adorable. Lisa and Ted are extremely happy on his arrival.

So follows the sleepless nights and exhausting days of child rearing. Steve is 2 years old and is busy playing with his toys. Seeing him being occupied, Lisa just decides to finish preparing his lunch, so she leaves him in the drawing room and goes to the kitchen. Steve generally plays with his toys and doesn't move away from them, but his attention is caught by the light, which is flickering on the electrical extension, and heads toward it to see it. Holding a colour pencil in his hand, he starts observing the light and also observes that there are certain sockets which are empty, so he decides to put the colour pencil in the empty socket.

In the meanwhile, Lisa just comes in the drawing room to check up on him, and is shocked to see what she saw. She rushes toward Steve and pulls him away from the extension board. She is relieved to be there on time and avoid a disaster, yet she can't help but feel guilty (UA: as a mother, I am supposed to protect my child). Steve is very upset that Mommy has interrupted his play (UA: you are supposed to give me what I want).

Steve is a brilliant child ahead of his game all the time even while playing with regular toys. He would just end up doing something more creative and impressive. Lisa would be happy and keep on encouraging him to do better (UA: it's my duty to bring out the best in my child). Steve would also respond to that and would better himself. Now Steve is old enough to go to school, and even in school, he is doing extremely well. Lisa and Ted are extremely proud by Steve's performance. Every time Steve would share his grades with Lisa, she would just smile and tell him that he has to do better than this next time. Steve would just stare at her face, smile back, and leave (<u>UA: You need to appreciate me enough</u>).

Story 2

The next story is about a family of Emma, Stephen, and their daughter, Sonia. Emma is a stay at home mom. Eventually, her parents stay with her so it's a big happy family. Sonia, right from her birth, got all the attention and adoration possible. Emma also ensured that Sonia gets everything she desires. In fact, she did not even pick up a job so that she could be for Sonia in every sense.

Almost after seven years, Emma and Stephen are expecting a second baby. Sonia is also very happy with the news. As she is learning more about the new baby, her enthusiasm increases. In the last few months, with the planning and the preparation for the new baby, Sonia gets a little uncomfortable as the focus has slightly moved from her to the new baby and its future requirements, but she is still eagerly waiting for the arrival of her baby brother.

Then comes the D-day and the baby is born. Yes, everybody is excited with the new arrival, but as the baby is brought home, the real challenge starts since Emma and Stephen are very much engaged with the new baby. Sonia starts to feel being ignored as the new baby has, for now, taken up all the attention and care, and both Emma and Stephen are exhausted to cater the needs of Sonia. Sonia knows she is not feeling good, but unable to understand how to articulate it. Once she falls sick and has to skip school, Emma ensures that she takes real good care of Sonia; and though it becomes difficult for Emma to manage, she still balances.

Sonia feels okay now, but as her health starts recovering, she notices that, again, the focus has been shifted from her to the new baby. Sonia again starts feeling bad (<u>UA: you need to give me the importance I deserve</u>). After a few days, Sonia again develops fever and stays back home. Now, Emma feels suspicious, as Sonia has always been a healthy baby. Emma notices this unusual behavior and due to her sensitive nature decides to address the problem at hand, so she sits Sonia down and starts explaining her how time and energy consuming it is to take care of new baby, and as a family, it's their duty to look after the baby and Sonia should understand this (<u>UA: since he is your sibling, you should love him</u>).

Story 3

This story is about Gina and Roy, who have raised their four sons and a daughter. Gina and Roy have a family business, which they are running successfully. As they are doing that, they are very sure that, eventually, their sons would join the business and help them grow the business to next level. Thus, they provided their sons with the best quality education (<u>UA: As we are parents we know what is best for our children</u>). And for their daughter, they were sure she would not have that kind of understanding or expertise, which is required for running a business. Hence, not a lot of attention was paid for her studies, but she was hardworking and had become independent. Very soon, she was keenly interested in entrepreneurship, so she took up a job and paid by herself for the management school, while the sons, though they got all the resources, they were not able to make the best of it as none of them had any inclination for business. So when time came for somebody to do the business, none of the sons deemed fit for the position. Also, the way they were given everything they required, they had become arrogant and irresponsible. Eventually, one by one, all the sons left their parent's house and went their own way. (UA: As loving parents, you should be okay with our life choices)

Now the businesses, as well as the parents, were left alone to deal with life, as they had no idea of what to do in the future and were very dejected by their son's behaviour. That's when their daughter stepped up and took charge of everything. Not only did she help them grow the business fifty times of what it was, but also took care of her parents in their old age.

Unspoken Agreements for Children:

1. You need to accept me and approve of me the way I am.
2. Being your parent, I know what's best for you.
3. As my parent, your love needs to be unconditional.
4. As my parent, you need to protect me.
5. As my children, you have to respect me.

6. As my parent, you have to be sensitive toward my feelings.
7. In spite of being my parent, you need to respect my space and choice.
8. As you are a parent (adult), you need to be perfect
9. As a parent, you need to demonstrate unconditional love.
10. As an adult, you cannot make mistakes (you have to know better)
11. Give me help when I ask for help
12. You should always give me the priority.
13. I can behave the way I want, but you always need to be at the best of your behavior.
14. You should love me more than you love anybody else.
15. You should fulfill all my desires.
16. You should always make me feel secure, care for me.
17. You should always appreciate me.
18. My happiness should be your happiness.
19. I always have a choice on what information about my life I need to share, but I would like to have all info about your life.

Unspoken Agreements for Parents:

1. I have a say in every decision of yours.
2. I know better than you.
3. Nobody can take my place in your life.
4. You have to respect me irrespective of anything.
5. Your business is my business.
6. I know what is best for you.

7. Your accomplishments are my accomplishments.
8. Your success is my success
9. I took care of you when you were young, and you take care of me when I am old.
10. You need to take care of me the way I took care of you.
11. I, as a parent can control your freedom.
12. As my child, you need to have empathy for me.
13. You cannot give my position in your life to anybody else.
14. You better fulfill my expectations.

CHAPTER 7

Unspoken Agreements in a Marriage

Marriage is the biggest unspoken agreement a human can make. A lot of beliefs, speculations, reasoning, and importance have been placed around this 'institution'. There are a lot of things, which determine success in a human life, and marriage seems to be the biggest parameter for a successful life. Though like any other arrangement, it has its own highlights and shortcomings; and it, in itself, is nothing. We have made it whatever it is.

Ultimate Level of Relationship

God created separation so that these two aspects come together, female and male. We all have these two aspects in us, and we seek for a partnership where these two can come together and can give us a complete experience.

Marriage is a culmination of two beings, an arrangement meant for benefits of each other and the society. We have somehow managed to complicate the hell out of it. We could have used it for evolution of our own self and the other person, but somehow, we have made it like one more obstacle for our growth by putting all kinds of restrictions possible on each other in the name of marriage—all the ideologies which have no definite source.

And now, we have all agreed with these ideas that from here, we are struggling to know what can we do to make it an enriching experience for any of us. Though from time to time we are reminded that love is what is really important in the same manner as it is in every relationship. Love is what drives willingness, which is very crucial for the success of a marriage.

Marriage seems to be the most important relationship in an individual's life, as it affects almost all aspects of the life, social, economical, personal, physical, mental, and so on. When we think, we say that, 'I want to make him/her mine.' As if he/she is a possession, which we can buy and make it belong to us. We forget that human is not material, and marriage is no arrangement of gaining complete rights/control over other person; and we fail to do so, we feel that this so-called institution of marriage doesn't work.

True love doesn't have these requirements. These are requirements of our ego. That's why we feel pain as we feel that we are losing control over other person. Joy is associated with love, and pain with ego. Marriage means creating a space for other person to express themselves freely, and if that person wants to share that space with you or not, it should again be that person's choice. In the same way you too have the same choice, and learn to coexist and enjoy each other completely.

If somebody loves us, it's not because of us, but the choice that other person has made. So we need to feel thankful for that choice, and we also should feel good about ourselves that we, too, let go of our insecurity, our own fears, our own ego, expose ourselves to this vulnerability willingly, and choose to love somebody outgrow our lack of ability to be selfless. Love and ego cannot exist together; thus, to experience true love, we have to drop our ego and the luxuries, which comes along with that.

Yet, a lot of emphasis lies around this concept of marriage like only if u stay in a marriage till u die then it is considered as a success. Maybe because this is one relationship, other than friendship, that you make out of choice; and if we make a wrong choice, that's how we deal with it, be it our fault or somebody else's. There is no way we can make a mistake (UA). It's like you want to reach office on time, and so you take a different route in an attempt to reach early, but apparently, you have reached late than you expected. So it was a mistake, now what do you do? Do u beat yourself up that how on earth u made this mistake, or do something to improve the mistake? So how is that choice, or any other choice, different from the choice you make during finding a life partner. And if you make a mistake in selecting a life partner, you live that mistake your entire life, or you do something to change that mistake??.

Marriage is an ego's requirement; true love does not need marriage. Hence, even if you have an intention of getting married, is it because you want to be for the other person? Then it is for love, but if it is for the other person to be for you, then it is for ego.

Story 1

One sunny day, Jim, as usual, got out for his morning walk. As he was jogging at his pace, he couldn't help notice things around, and then started focusing his thoughts on his day and all the things he is supposed to do the next day. As he got lost in his thoughts, he slightly gazed on his left hand side toward the garden, and saw a girl with her eyes closed under the tree deep in meditation. As he continued jogging, he just couldn't get his eyes off her, as their was an amazing sense of peace emanating from her face, which was very magnetic. He stopped there just so he could enjoy this sight. Before he could realise half an hour had passed, he reluctantly left the place promising himself that he would return next day to the place.

The whole day, even at work, he couldn't get her out of his head. He kept convincing himself that it's just a matter of few hours, and once again, he will be in front of her.

Next morning, as he reached the place, his eyes desperately kept looking for her but in vain. She couldn't be seen anywhere. Jim was utterly disappointed, as he never thought that he wouldn't able to see her again. He still convinces himself with all kinds of stories and excuses of why she was not present that day. Then finally telling himself that he would very soon see her again.

Months passed, and everyday, Jim would go to the park without missing a single day just with the hope of seeing her again, but with no luck. Finally, one day at his office party, Jim was stunned to see the face he had been searching everywhere. There she was, across the room, looking fabulous in a beautiful pink silk evening gown. Jim just kept staring at her, completely blank. Then in a flash, a thought popped in his head. 'I have to talk to her.'

Somehow, as he gained his senses back, he slowly started walking toward her. She was busy chatting with other people. As he got closer, his mouth went dry and heart beating at a rate of ten miles per hour. He reached close to her, and she looked at him with a warm welcoming smile and said, 'Hi, I am Jenny.' Jim continued staring. She repeated her 'hi', raising her voice a bit, and that broke Jim's trance. He mustered courage to reply back then as they got talking, they immediately hit it off. Jenny, too, enjoyed Jim's company and stayed with him throughout the party. They called it a night with exchange of numbers, and with a commitment of meeting again. That was just the beginning. It wasn't too long before they fell madly in love with each other, and within a year, they had decided to get married.

The first year of marriage was just bliss. They both were also doing very well with their careers. Jenny, apparently, was more successful than Jim, though it never seemed to bother him. But now, Jenny had gotten promoted. She was the new director of the company, and as per the demands of the new role, she was travelling more than usual.

Initially, Jim was very supportive of her, but as he was getting frustrated with his job, he had started missing Jenny being around, as he had nobody to share his woes with (<u>UA: I am happy for your success but you should also be around if I need you</u>). Slowly, this frustration started turning into bitterness for Jim, as even if Jenny was around, he would still be distant with her and start picking fights with her over small matters. Jenny kept struggling to understand the real issue, as she really wanted to help Jim (<u>UA: if you need</u>

my help, you should ask for it and let me help you), but Jim had now reached a point where his resentment was beyond help. And Jenny was also losing her patience between her job and Jim's changing behaviour. Love is never a problem, it's the role we assume in each relationship and the ideologies around those roles, which we accept and believe without challenging it.

Story 2

Keith is a shy, romantic at heart, and passionate in nature. He does work, but not with an intention of earning money or driven to prove himself, but with pure liking for the job where he writes articles for papers and magazines. He has a very unique style of his own to address the modern issues, which, at times, gets a little controversial, but he manages to somehow make it easy to digest without affecting the seriousness of the issue, and ensuring that the reader does get the message.

Rose is somewhat similar to him in nature, but she is a little more practical than Keith. Being a kindergarten teacher, she tends to be a little more than irritable, as it is not something she would like to do, but has to compromise doing it as she has convinced herself that this is all she can do, as she has no inclination to find out where her true passion lies. Now, they have been married for four years just after knowing each other for not more than six months. They have enjoyed a perfect partnership right from sharing household responsibilities to financial demands, but for them, it did feel right.

Lately Rose's frustration has increased more than usual, as she tends to get a little jealous with Keith who does his work with so much of ease, and ends up getting everything one desires from their work (i.e., money, appreciation, satisfaction). Though Rose really loves Keith and so does he, it didn't affect them till now, but things have changed for Rose in school. There has been a new principal who has been appointed and is giving Rose a really hard time. Initially, Rose would share her issues with Keith, but now, even she is tired of complaining and somehow expects Keith to ask her about her issues (<u>UA: being my husband, you should be sensitive and intuitive enough to know about my troubles, and not expect me to every time talk about it on my own</u>).

Keith has also been busy because holidays are close, and there has been too much of demand for Keith's work. Since Rose's unexpected silence didn't reveal much, he, too, assumed that all's well with her (<u>UA: if you have an issue, you will talk to me about it</u>). In spite of all the love Rose has for Keith, she has started being resentful, as she is self-loathing and drowning in her own sorrows, and has convinced herself that Keith doesn't love her anymore as he is not paying required attention to her. This has started creating rift between Keith and Rose.

Story 3

Vicky and Tina have been married for more than two years now. Their parents had been friends forever, and they somehow were amused by the idea of getting their children married, as that would take their friendship to the next level. Though Vicky and Tina had known each other since childhood, they, too, were fond of each other, but were not so much convinced if they loved each other. They did share a very good level of comfort and understanding, so as this marriage thing was proposed, they did not feel much of a need to resist and decided to go with the flow.

Life is good for both of them, as they are doing well for themselves in their careers, and everything is very comfortable with minimal need for drama. Though despite of this comfort, they both miss that spark or the excitement of what it would be like falling in love, feeling where you are completely swept off your feet.

As life progressed, they both have gotten okay with this feeling of lack, and decided within themselves to settle for what they have. They convinced themselves that they have what more than many people would just dream of having. Now, as they are dealing with this situation, Tina has learnt that she is pregnant and they both have taken this news in the happiest way possible. Vicky has also been very responsible and totally participating as he can, so after a few months, Tina delivers a beautiful baby boy, Matthew. They both get busy with taking care of this big shift in their life; hence, striking balance between their personal and professional life.

Life thus seems perfect, as they literally have nothing to complain about. Once, as Tina is dropping Matthew off to his preschool, she bumps into one of her old school friend, Bill, who is also there to see off his niece. They both get to talking and end up spending hours catching up. Tina comes back home with Matthew, but somehow, she is still thinking about her day with Bill. As she is lost in thoughts, suddenly her phone flashes, and Vicky is calling her. When she comes back to her senses, she feels extremely guilty, as she is reminded of the fact that she is married and this is wrong of her to feel this way about anybody else than her husband (<u>UA: in a marriage, it's not right to feel good about spending time with somebody, who can be your potential partner, other than your spouse</u>). She pulls herself back and answers the phone with a lot of hesitation, thus, promising herself that she would not allow herself to feel like this ever.

So now, she has started avoiding dropping Matthew to his preschool, as she feels she cannot face Bill and the best way to avoid the situation is by running away from it completely. But at times if she would pick up Matthew, she would secretly wish to see Bill at least from a distance, and would feel disappointed if that would not happen. On the other hand, Vicky does suspect something as he can notice change in Tina's behaviour, but is hesitant to initiate a conversation as he doesn't know what that confrontation would do to their marriage (<u>UA: you should always protect the sanctity of the marriage</u>). Secretly, he does miss their friendship before marriage where they could freely discuss anything they want without any worries, as the space of comfort has been lost.

Unspoken Agreements in Marriage:

1. Infidelity in a marriage only is qualified if one of the spouse engages in a physical relationship with somebody else.
2. Marriage is the end of all issues, and the final destination of a romantic affair.

3. Marriage is the only way you can celebrate your relationship.
4. There needs to be mutual understanding and unconditional love all the time in the marriage.
5. For a successful marriage, both need to stay together.
6. You have to look after each other, and take care of each other.
7. You need to honour and fulfill each other's wishes.
8. It has to be regarded as the most important relationship in life.
9. Each other's families also have to be given their share of respect and acceptance.
10. The success of a marriage is based on its longevity.
11. You cannot allow yourself to fall in love with anybody else.
12. All your needs have to be fulfilled in the marriage.
13. Your spouse has to be your soulmate.
14. For a woman, even if she is professionally successful, her true success is considered if she is a good wife or a mother.
15. For a man, even if he is really good at being a husband or a father, his true success is considered only if he is professionally good.
16. Marriage is full of compromises.
17. It's ideal to be married to have children to provide them with a stable environment.
18. To settle in life, marriage is crucial.
19. If your marriage doesn't work, then it means you are a failure no matter what you have to make your marriage work.

20. Marriage is sacred and ultimate; one can experience the other person is yours in every sense if you would marry her/him (ultimate possession/ultimate sense of belonging).
21. The rules in the marriage have to be followed.
22. You cannot be married and feel free to make choices.
23. Children make marriage stronger.
24. It's more important to stay in a marriage than staying happy being alone, and so on.

CHAPTER 8

Unspoken Agreements in Profession

One of the aspects of our life through which we derive our value is the work we do and the success/failure we experience in that. Our profession not just helps us earn money, but also plays a pivotal role in what we think about ourselves. Dissatisfaction in the work we do can result into serious depression or even identity crisis. Having said that, it's again our own attitude toward our work irrespective of what we do, which can makes us feel good about it.

Once I was waiting for a friend at the end of a road that was getting constructed. She was taking too long, and I couldn't help but notice the workers doing the laborious tasks. The interesting thing was that though all were doing the same work, their faces were telling different stories. I noticed this one worker who was sighing continuously, stopping, getting irritated on his fellow workers, taking break to rest, then again reluctantly completing the task. I approached him and asked, 'What are you doing?' To which he replied rudely, 'Can't you see I am putting sand?' I backed off.

Next, I noticed this another worker who silently was doing his job, though he was not as physically strong as the previous person, but he was quite diligently completing the task. I asked him what he was doing, and he lifted his head slightly and said, 'I am constructing a road.' And he got back to what he was doing. I finally started moving away from that site, as I thought I saw my friend's car. Then I noticed this one worker who was singing, chatting away with his co-workers, helping them, and also ensuring that everything was done properly, though it was not his responsibility to do so. I first though he must be the contractor, but then I saw him doing the same work as others were doing, so I thought I'd ask him the same question. As I approached him, without even saying anything, he looked at me, smiled, and prompted me to stand back as there was a lot of dust. As the dust settled, I asked him, 'What are you doing?' To which he stood up with his chest puffed and said, 'I am paving way for a better life.'

He continued explaining to me how after the sand, there will be sprinkling of water and other details of constructing the road. He also ended up telling me how he works for more that fourteen hours, how its his dream to make his son a doctor, and how he is determined he will accomplish his dream. As I got engrossed in the conversation, I could hear my friend calling out to me from a distance. I left that site learning so much about attitude, intention, and motivation, and how you can easily derive it through the work you do.

Story 1

Janine started her career at a very young age, as she had lost her parents in a car accident and was survived by two siblings. In spite of having tough times ahead of her, Janine fought against all odds and worked for a small training company with limited prospects. At that point of time, it was the question of survival, but she didn't treat her job as work and gave all her efforts. In fact, she enrolled herself in different kinds of courses, which she felt would help her with her work and would benefit the company too.

Due to her foresightedness and vision, she was able to support her company to grow in an unimaginable manner. She was one of the twenty employees who had joined the company in its beginning days, and now, it almost had two thousand people working for it. Obviously, Janine was promoted and was in the top directorial level. Also, on the personal front, she had done an excellent job in settling her siblings in their respective lives.

The day Janine got the announcement of her promotion, she was extremely thrilled and felt like she had received the best token of appreciation. After a month or so of her being in this new role, she started realising that the role was not exciting her in the way she expected it to. Though it was a lot of money and perks, those things did not seem to matter any more, as she had started missing the drive she used to get out of the interactions with the clients, and how each time the excitement she would feel when she would do the training.

Gradually, it had become a drag for her to go to work as her interest had slowly getting deteriorated (<u>UA: my work is supposed to give me the excitement I am looking for</u>), and she couldn't identify herself any more with her new role. But she was finding it difficult to even quit the job, as she felt like she had earned what she had got and quitting would mean like throwing away all that she had worked for (<u>UA: life doesn't count for anything without the accomplishments you earn</u>).

Unspoken Agreements in a Professional Set-Up:

1. Professional success is very important for me to feel successful as an individual.
2. For me to succeed, somebody has to fail.
3. Success means either the position or the achievement of the targets given.
4. Ratings determine whether I am good at my work or not.
5. My passion and profession may not be the same.
6. You cannot be emotional in your professional space.
7. Certain codes of conduct needs to be followed if you want to be professionally successful.
8. You have to be competitive to shine in your professional space.
9. I should not allow myself to feel too comfortable with where I stand currently, or else, somebody will surpass me.
10. Life is a race.
11. You have to be different than who you are in your personal life.
12. I should feel threatened by every potential competitor.
13. There is no substitute for hard work.

14. The top of the pinnacle is always scarce.
15. If I need to be successful, I have to be good at everything I do.
16. I will start enjoying my life once I retire.
17. It's okay if, as a human being, I don't do the right thing as long as I am a good professional.
18. I am working for somebody else.
19. Good education can help me build a good career.
20. Working is all about earning money.
21. Being ruthless/aggressive helps you become successful.
22. Its easy for you to be successful if you come from a successful family.
23. You don't need to be talented as long as your dad/ mom have a good successful running business/ company.

CHAPTER 9

Unspoken Agreement with God

The way we understand love of God is the way we understand love around us, which is judgmental and conditional, and also based on what we receive in the name of love. In our current lives, we don't have a single relationship in our life, including our relationship with our own self, which we can compare to the love of God, as it is the purest and most unconditional love one can experience. I would still make a poor attempt to explain this by comparing bits and pieces of every relationship we, as humans, experience in our world.

God's love can be compared to the love of a mother who will go through the pain of watching her baby fall and get hurt and still not stop her child, as she knows that this skill of walking is what her baby will need for the rest of her life to live an independent life. Or God's love can be compared to the love of the lover who, when sees that his object of affection is going away from him, would still not stop her, as he genuinely would want her to find her happiness and would just patiently keep waiting for her to come back to him and continue loving her the way she wants. Or maybe God's love can be compared to the love of a friend where a friend may not agree with all the choices her friend is making for herself, but will continue supporting her and being with her through all her endeavors. Or God's love can be compared to a brother's love who, to protect his sister, would stand in front of his angry dad and take the beating on her behalf. God's love can also be compared to a guru's love where a guru would show his disciple the path on which to walk to attain what he wants, but would honor his choice to tread on the same path or not.

So basically, whenever you have experienced any form of unconditional love, either you have given somebody that kind of love or you have had the fortune to receive that kind of love. Just understand God's love is 10,000 times of that. And if we feel we don't experience this love, then the only reason is our ignorance and inability to recognize the same.

As somewhere we want to believe that we are alone otherwise how would we justify all the suffering of our life because if we believe there is a supreme protector then he may not be doing a good job on protecting his loved ones and punishing those who harm them. This is what we generally perceive of God. But the thing is that we were created in image of God so all the powers he has to change our lives he already has blessed us with those, in fact no matter what challenges we face in life we have all the resources to turn it around, our life is purely our creation, the one we created through our individual thoughts and also collective thoughts. What we see around us and are unhappy about are, things that are a projection of our idea of world. There is no point in waiting around for somebody else to take responsibility to change world, we all right now by living a conscious life can start doing it.

CHAPTER 10

Significance of Emotions and States of Mind

Emotion can be regarded as nothing but energy in motion. If we understand this well then a lot of things can become simple. With all our life experiences we at least know till now that being happy or peaceful is what we all aspire for and actually this is our natural state, being stressed and worried is not natural for us, we have learnt to do so over a period of time either by mimicking others or by falsely believing that to reach somewhere in life we need to be this way.

Being peaceful is organic while being stressed or fearful is toxic.

Lets me explain this with the help of an example:

Its like trying to swim in an upstream, if any of you have experienced this then you may agree that the effort and the energy required will be way more than if you swim in a downstream. The act of swimming is same but both the experiences will be very different from each other. So to conclude if we do things, which don't feel natural to us then by the end of the day, it is going to leave us exhausted and tired. Here I cannot stress more on the point that situations are not causing those emotions inside of us but we are choosing to get affected and react to those situations then respond to them, as they are not our natural body responses.

Body is just taking instructions from us and we are making it toil hard, cause of our obliviousness.

Emotions are like entities. All human experiences are constituted of various emotions, beliefs, ideas, thoughts, opinions, judgments, and insights. These factors determine the quality of our experience. We decide which emotion to attach to which experience. We worship one more than other.

Emotion emerges from the mind/soul while feeling emerge from the body. That's why most of the people who have a near-death experience (NDE) normally report experiencing pure love, absolute forgiveness, and pure wisdom. Not being in their physical form does not stop them from embracing their true nature, which is pure bliss.

Lets further understand on how to take charge of our lives with the help of creating emotions

Being Responsible is Really Empowering

To change anything in our lives, first we need to take responsibility for it. To create any kind of change, no matter how big or small it is, the first step toward making any kind of change is to take responsibility of the situation. It's like taking ownership of the current situation. And to make any kind of change, we need to own up for the plight of the current situation. Also, taking responsibility does not mean to put the blame on someone or something, or to put blame on even yourself. Positive change can be created only from the space of responsibility, and not from the space of blame.

We should understand before we complain/criticise others that people cannot behave the way you want all the time.

All the big leaders the earth has ever seen have worked from the space of responsibility and not blame. They have taken charge of their emotions, and chosen the best ones to help them handle their challenges. That's how they were able to create a meaningful shift of some kind. Responsibility provides us with amazing freedom, thus, enabling us to do anything we wish. What we give, we receive more!

Lets know that if we show understanding and acceptance in all our relationships, chances are we will receive more of the same as well. But here, many people would say that we have done that but it doesn't work. So here, the real question is did u do it from the space of love or fear? Any action done from the space of love will not generate resentment or blame.

Blaming means:

- we feel somebody else is responsible for the situation
- hence, we don't do anything about it
- hence, nothing changes
- thus, making us feel powerless and helpless

Every time we make an assumption, we fail in our communication

Now let's understand more about different aspects of emotions, which creates our personality and our attitude in general.

Beingness or Awareness or Consciousness

These are nothing but our state of mind to which we connect most prominently, which in return constitutes our personality. This states can also be a strong influence on our attitude; hence, shaping our overall experience of life.

There are certain levels of beingness:

1. Peace/bliss
2. Love
3. Surrender
4. Acceptance
5. Forgiveness
6. Assertiveness
7. Guilt/Blame
8. Loneliness
9. Pleasure
10. Victimising
11. Fear

The thing is that we keep on fluctuating among these levels of emotions and spend more time at a certain level than others. As we have also seen that more time we spend on feeling a certain emotion or delve in certain thought that ultimately becomes the focal point of all our life experiences.

Most of us spend our lives focused on the lower levels (i.e., of surviving, exploring, and seeking all kinds of sensory pleasures possible). This does not happen out of choice, but out of ignorance, as we don't know how much is enough to survive—we fail to draw that line.

It's mostly after a difficult situation we realise that life means more than just merely existing. For example, a doctor doing well in his career focused on earning money treats his patient from sense of duty than willingness, but when that same doctor encounters a situation where his son is diagnosed with learning disabilities, his whole perspective toward healing changes, and eventually he may choose to run a healing centre for children with learning disabilities, as now he can actually empathize with the parents and children who are in the similar situation.

Sometimes we need a slight jerk in life to understand our true potential, but I would say don't wait till then if possible, start the internal change from this very moment, as you don't always need to fail to enjoy your success.

The Concept of Core Energy

Life is about finding your passion and making every moment count and living to its fullest. And to do that, it's important for us to understand where our core energy lies.

We all have our core energy centres from which we derive energy and the drive for all other things we do. For some, it's their work. For some, it's relationships. For some, it's the place they live in or are associated with. For some, it's their appearance. This core energy serves like a fundamental reservoir of energy for us. We can compare this to the dominoes concept. The core energy centre is like when the first domino is toppled, the rest of the dominoes just topple from there on.

This is from where we get our main motivation to do things in life. This energy centre also defines us. It helps us get or even strengthen our sense of identity.

Core Energy Centre:

1. <u>Knowledge-centric core:</u> when you are completely driven by gaining information and learning about new things, concepts.
2. <u>Creativity-centric core:</u> when somebody is driven by creative work, may be like artists, musicians, or any kind of creative stimulating work.
3. <u>Love/relationships:</u> some people thrive on idea of romance and entirely derive their energy from relationships of all sorts.
4. <u>Power:</u> some of us are status-driven where we engage in activities which gives us a sense of power and control, and idea of losing it can totally disrupt our engagement with life.
5. <u>Work:</u> there are also some of us who gain all the happiness with the work they do, professionally or personally as well.
6. <u>Pleasure:</u> while there are some who are completely motivated by indulging in things/activities which brings all kinds of sensory pleasures.
7. <u>Adventure:</u> there are also some who love to live on edge and are driven by the moments of complete rush, as it can give them a sense of being truly alive like mountaineers, hikers.

8. <u>Need to help/caring:</u> well then, there are some who believe in changing the world and are motivated by being as helpful as they can for others like social activists.

9. <u>Healing work:</u> then we also have people who dedicate their lives just toward healing others, and are all engaged in helping people live better lives like doctors, holistic healers.

There can be other core energy centers as well along with those mentioned above. So it would be helpful to find out what is our personal core energy center as, if one is feeling lost in life or depressed then it may be helpful to explore where your true drive for life emerges from and you can develop that. Along with helping yourself by becoming aware of your core energy center this idea can also help you understand people around you in a better way specially those with whom you have relationships. It's the core energy that drives the willingness or unwillingness to do something.

The common, belief is that the true purpose of life is to achieve the milestones set by us. For example, as a child we need to study, then we need to have a great career, later get married, have kids, have a healthy body or a fit body, and so on; and we are expected to not just achieve these milestones, but also to be successful in each one of these, and the success will be determined with the end result. We have identified ourselves so much with this reality that if in anyone of these aspects we don't reach the standard of success again set by others, we are quick enough to consider ourselves as failures.

Parents should teach their children that result is just one factor, but that's not the only thing that matters. They really need to enjoy what they are doing, need to be sincere in their efforts, and be honest with themselves. These are the factors, which will make them feels as a success. Our obsession with perfection is what drives us to be so result-oriented, whereas the whole concept of perfection is a big lie in itself.

We have learned to live our life based on the result we achieve and by the superficial standards set for success, and thus, we end up feeling frustrated and pressurised all the time. Is life really about being successful or about being your best in every circumstance? Best does not mean *perfect*. Your best is never going to be the same from one moment to the next. Sometimes, your best will mean to be most efficient, and other times it would mean to be most patient. Your self-definition of being best cannot be when you're healthy as opposed to sick, feeling happy, or upset. Regardless of the quality, keep doing your best. When you overdo, you deplete yourself; and when you do less than your best, you subject yourself to self-judgement, guilt, and regrets. Support and encourage yourself. If you're happy with your response in every situation it can be considered you being at your best which is more important than being "perfect".So lets take the control back in our hands and create our own definition of "success" or "perfection".

If you do your best always, you will become a master of transformation. Think about it, We adopt a certain behaviour, which gives us the result we expect. Like for example, some people get angry over everything because they feel that other people just respond to them when they exhibit this behaviour, while some will always complain or crib to get what they want. The interesting thing here is you may get, for that time being, the result you hope for, but this behaviour of yours is also affecting your whole well-being. We become what we say and we think. So even unconsciously don't choose behaviour, which is not benefitting you in long run.

As mentioned in this book, law of attraction works on emotion, so if there is a certain emotion you are feeling more than others, chances are that you will end up attracting more situations which will make you feel more of that emotion.

To be able to reach anywhere in life, it's very crucial to be thankful/grateful for where you are right now no matter how difficult or bad your present circumstance you consider it to be. Find something to be grateful about in this situation, as it's like taking first step towards a better future /experiences.

Always remember you are always bigger than any of your experience of life. After all, experience is nothing but succession of events, and we give it any importance it holds.

How we cause suffering for ourselves?

- By comparison
- By unwilling sacrifices
- By being rigid about ideas and beliefs about how others should behave
- By having expectations and being attached to them

How we can end suffering for ourselves?

- Sacrifice should be done only when it does not feel like a sacrifice.
- Charity should be done only when it does not feel like a charity.

- Forgiveness should be given only when it does not feel like you are doing it for the other person but for yourself.
- Help should be given only when it does not feel like a help

We create unspoken agreement, also with emotions like trust, love, hope, satisfaction, we create various stories in our minds of what it is like experience 'love' in relationship, or what is like to experience 'satisfaction' in a job. These are all our impressions that we create of what it is, how it is to be experienced, and what it means if only expressed in a certain manner. For example, we all talk about 'satisfaction in job, but how many of us know exactly what it means, as it varies with every person who experiences it? Also for instance, we are doing our dream job, doing the same thing every day over and over again, and no perks or appreciation. Then even the dream job can end up being a drag, as we are expected to tweak our definition of satisfaction and how we need to experience it. Having said that, true satisfaction will always come from within. So even if you want to create a story about these abstract things, create those who will benefit you and help you experience the real thing then running around in circles. There is nothing, which we cannot turn around, be situation, experience or emotion.

The next emotion we will talk about is feeling betrayed, when somebody breaks our trust. We need to understand that when we say 'I trust you', we are kind of burdening the other person with the responsibility of keeping our trust, whereas we secretively have a hidden agenda of protecting ourselves against the unknown, and we are clear in our own mind of how this has to be expressed which that person may be aware of or not. For example, if a thief mugs somebody, he wouldn't be blamed for breaking the trust of the person he mugged as there were no expectations or 'right' expectation. Expectations kill relationships, whereas acceptance helps bloom relationships. Even when someone says 'I care for you', the expectation is that it would be reciprocated, or the other person should be obligated about. Hence, we develop these unspoken agreements with every emotion we know, and then it leads to disappointments. Let's have it, but again not projected without but within.

'I trust myself.'
'I care for myself.'
'I respect myself.'
'I honor myself.'
'I appreciate myself.'
'I forgive myself.'

Let's start doing it for ourselves before, as it becomes our second nature. This is the right thing, which we can do for others without holding any unspoken agreement for them, and so enjoy fulfilling relationships with others and ourselves.

Just choose the right emotion, and we are good to go.

Below is the beautiful basket of emotions from which you can choose:

Emotion type	Emotion words (drawn from the list in Appendix 2)
Admiration	Admiration, impressed, esteem
Amusement	Amused, entertained, gaiety, merry, playful, humorous, glee, funny, laughing, jolly
Anticipation	Anticipation, eager, expectant
Confidence	Confident, assurance, secure, trust
Courage	Courageous, brave, heartened
Desire	Desire, attracted, ardent, longing, craving, yearning, nostalgic
Dreaminess	Dreamy, contemplative, pensive
Enchantment	Enchanted, awe, charmed, moved, touched, enthrallment, wonder
Energized	Energetic, exuberant, zest, active, excited, stimulated
Euphoria	Euphoric, rapture, ecstasy, exaltation, thrilled, elated, high, exhilaration, exultation, jubilant, enraptured
Fascination	Fascinated, interest, curious, inquisitive, attentive, engrossed
Hope	Hope, optimistic, encouraged, wishful
Inspiration	Inspiration, enthusiasm, tempted, determined, challenged, zeal
Joy	Joy, bliss, overjoyed, pleasure, happy, good, delighted, wonderful, rejoice, smile, cheerful, enjoyment
Kindness	Kind, caring, friendly, tenderness, warm
Love	Love, romantic, infatuation, sentimental, fondness, in love, liking, affection, intimate
Lust	Lust, horny, passion, aroused, sensual, sexy
Pride	Pride, triumphant, self-satisfaction, smug
Relaxation	Relaxed, at peace, at ease, comfortable, peaceful, lighthearted, carefree, placid, serene, tranquil, easygoing, calm
Relief	Relief, reassured, gratitude, soothed, thankful
Respect	Respect, appreciating, approve
Satisfaction	Satisfaction, gratified, pleased, contentment, fulfilled, glad
Surprise	Surprise, amazement, astonished, startled, dazzled
Sympathy	Sympathy, compassion, empathy, pity, understanding, forgiving
Worship	Worship, adoration, devotion, reverence

CHAPTER 11

'Flow with whatever is happening, and let your mind be free. Stay centered by accepting whatever you are doing.
This is the ultimate.'

– Chuang Tzu

The following are different ways to work with self, which would in return help us deal better with the unspoken agreements:

1. Self-Intervention:

Think of one person with whom you want to change the dynamics of your relationship in a positive sense. Tell yourself the reason of your disappointment and now complete the following sheet:

<u>Worksheet: This worksheet is very helpful for us to not just become aware of UA but also finally be able to forgive and understand the other person.</u>

1. What is . . . supposed to do?
    (Write the name of the person in the blanks) and answer the question.

    ....

2. What am/was I supposed to do?
    (Make a note of what you think your action could be/have been) and write it below.

    ....

3. Name the emotion you are feeling right now.
    (It could be one or more than one, list all of them)

    ....

4. Are you open to the idea to feel an emotion more comfortable/peaceful
    (You can choose to answer either YES or NO. Then it means you are still unwilling to forgive the other person, then I would suggest pick another person for now and again start with question1)

    ....

5. What could probably be the UA?
    (State in your words what possibly is the UA you are
    dealing with here, and if you could also try and guess
    what the other person's UA could have been, by doing
    this we can get a quick resolution)

    ....

6. Now say this power statement to yourself: 'I am
    releasing myself and the <u>other person</u>* of this UA"(state
    the UA)*(Name of the person)
    (Say it out loud and as you are saying it notice the
    emotion within, and if the emotion is still negative then
    we have to keep saying it till the time we don't change
    it to a positive/neutral emotion, if you face difficulties
    in doing so first think of a Higher power* and ask for
    help and second use the process where we stress on one
    word and say the above statement, to understand how
    to do this better check out last chapter of the book, also
    make a note that first time when you say you may state
    the UA but if you need to repeat then just say the power
    statement, your brain is smart enough to know what you
    are doing and will help you with the same)
    *Higher power could be anything from the God you
    believe to nature or your values, anything which you
    regard to be superior

    ....

7. Terminate the unspoken agreement by writing this on a piece of paper, then either throw it away or dispose in a way which would give you a feeling of release.

    ....

8. Make a note of your emotion.

    ....

9. Create a new agreement with yourself, which would make you feel liberated rather than bounded.
    (Write the new agreement)

    ....

10. Declare it.(If possible tell somebody about it, like your best friend/spouse/anybody whom you feel like)

    ....

There are more worksheets attached at the end of the book. Do complete as many worksheets as possible.

2. Self-Annihilation: This process is for you to release yourself of all the labels you have given to yourself and understand that none of these roles have the ability to define you so do fulfill all your responsibilities but from the space of detachment, be involved with life but don't identify with anything. As doing that can help us breeze through life then put self-inflicting pressure to fulfill the responsibilities of our roles in life.

What do I derive my self-worth from? Or my self-importance like my job or the degree I carry or the possessions I have or the people I have around me, yet all this identification is so fragile as everything in there can change, hence, leaving you question your self-worth?

Process of Self-Annihilation:

Look for a quiet spot, relax your whole body starting from your toes. As you breathe in, imagine your toe getting relaxed with every breathe out. Now move your attention to your feet. Again, follow the same steps, slowly move to your legs, then stomach, then to hands, neck, and simultaneously relax your whole body As you notice your breathing going in and out of your body, start thinking of the question, 'Who am I?' And as your mind will start answering this question, imagine that answer in a call-out placed at a certain distance from your body, and now, with every answer, imagine such call-outs being placed all around your body. As your mind will exhaust the answers, just do a quick review of all the answers. Now, focus on one call-out each time, and see as you focus your attention to one, it's bursting out like a bubble. See all the call-outs turning into bubble till the last call-out gets burst. Now pause and notice how you feel. Initially, you may feel a little uncomfortable and scary, but being in this state, just notice what emerges from here. Notice the lightness you will start feeling in your entire being, and think of one word to explain this state to yourself. You can use this word as a reference whenever you feel like experiencing this state again.

Image of call-out around body:

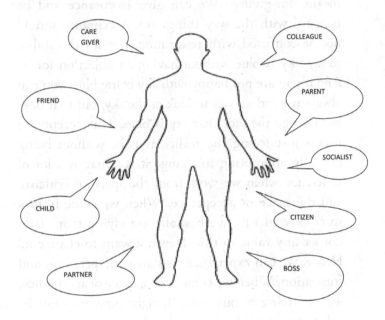

3. Self-Coherence

> 'to understand everything is to forgive everything'.
>
> —Buddha

Two important aspects to bring in inner coherence are

1. Forgiveness: Total acceptance. Forgiveness in itself means 'for-giving'. We can give acceptance and be peaceful with the way things are. Acceptance should not be confused with resignation, but it's the ability to say 'sky is blue without having an objection for it'. And if you are not happy with sky being blue, you can always use red glasses to look at the sky, but that does not change the fact that sky is blue. True acceptance means just seeing the reality as it is, without being critically attempting to change it, as there is a lot of difference when we work from the space of criticism and the space of acceptance. When we come from a space of criticism, we basically are saying that, 'I do not see any value in this. Hence, I want to change it.' Hence, we can experience resistance, desperation, and frustration. When we come from a space of acceptance, we are saying to ourselves, 'I, right now, may not be able to see any value in this, but I am sure there is and I want to make it better.' Hence, there would be peace and patience as you attempt to change it. This can be an act of altruism. As we learn to forgive others, our expectations from others are lowered. Hence, we feel more at peace and freedom from within.

The points regarding forgiveness:

- When it comes to forgiveness, we realize that forgiving some people is easier while it's difficult to forgive some.
- But given the nature of our mind is that, the way we do something is the way we do everything
- Also knowing the fact that our brain is plastic in nature so what we focus on shall increase
- In my experience every single person in our life has somehow disappointed us, of course some more than others, and many a time these incidents are even forgotten by us until once again if somebody behaves in a way which hurts us, all that was forgotten is remembered and our mind, like an efficient defense lawyer, is capable of creating a strong case against the other person.
- Thus when we really want to start forgiving, we should start from the person who is very dear to us and forgiving them is easy and then gradually moving on to the people whom we really find difficult to forgive.

2. Free of Judgement: We, as humans, are taught to be judgemental as a part of our need to survive. But life is not about surviving but of experiencing it in its full glory. Mostly, all the times our fear of self-preservation is what compels us to judge almost everything around us. Sometimes, this does help us in protecting ourselves, but we do spend a lot of time just feeling anxious and worried; thus, losing out on the experience of being

spontaneous. Nothing can be completely judged as good or bad. With a change in the perspective or situation, the dynamics around good and bad also changes; hence, what we may consider as the worst experience can be shown to have some good part in it. So the idea is to refrain ourselves from getting into judgement and sometimes just be an observer and see/notice a thing as it is without any need of categorising it, as sometimes, we even don't like things that we don't understand or have limited knowledge about. We have to consciously let go of our need for people to meet our benchmark of right/wrong or anything we believe, as only we aware of the benchmark we have created. Other person has no idea about that. Judgements clog our ability to see things as it is. The real art of living a judgement-free life is to learn to be involved in everything around us, but not identifying with anything. Either everything seems good around us or everything seems bad completely depends on our own state of mind, and it is always our choice to let outer situations influence our inner state of mind and the way we would perceive world around us. Along with the judgements, we also end up making a lot of assumptions to support our judgement; hence, making things worse. So we should learn to inculcate the habit of keeping our judgements at bay and rely on matters of fact. What if there is no good or bad in this world? We just experience what we create! So see what you have created. If you are not completely satisfied with what you have got, then change it. And if changing is not possible for you, then administer the choice of changing the way you feel about it, as it, again, will create the experience you wanted in the first place. Is it really that simple? Well, we really need to ask ourselves this question as we all have our own answer for it.

For instance, let's talk about pain. The minute somebody hears pain, we immediately want to relieve it or discard it or curb it, and somehow manage to avoid it, as pain is 'bad' for most of us. While there are some of us who will create pain deliberately, either for themselves or others, some might think why would we do that? Always remember, 'Every behaviour, action adopted benefits the doer in his/her experience of life in some way or other.'

One may always be aware of those benefits or not is a different question altogether. Even now, for a lot of people reading this, they mostly have decided in their heads of what is good or bad and not just regarding pain but about everything they encounter. So what's the verdict? Is pain good or bad? And the answer to that is that 'Pain is just pain'. How you choose to relate to that experience of pain determines it for you as good or bad. Our judgements continue with ourselves as well. We are constantly judging ourselves; hence, scrutinising our every action/word/thought. Most of the times this is an attempt to feel good about our self. We need a frame of reference in order to know who we are or how 'good' we are. This method may help us in some way, but overall, it's an exhausting process and not an enjoyable one.

Let's do a small exercise:

Share an experience you feel strongly about. Now notice how you feel about it. Next, explain the same experience, but this time, try to state the event as it is without attaching any meaning or emotion to it. Notice how you feel. For instance:

Example 1:

When I was of age six, my mum planned my birthday, and I was pretty excited about it as I was expecting it to be celebrated at this new theme park, which had just opened close to our house. I had dropped enough hints for her to know that I would really love to spend my birthday at the park. So on the D-day, I hopefully kept on waiting for her to ask me to go out with her, but she seemed just busy in the kitchen. As day progressed, my anxiety kept on increasing. I struggled to assuage it, but my efforts went in vain, and I finally declared to myself that my birthday has been ruined. Then all of a sudden, my friends arrived at my house with gifts, as my mother had thrown a surprise birthday party for me, inviting all my friends in order to celebrate the special day. I still was not sure of whether I was happy or disappointed. As I saw my mother attending to all my friends, my dejection just went on increasing. Although I ended up celebrating my birthday in the most ideal way, I was still not too pleased with it.

Now try reading the same story skipping/modifying the words of emotions like excited/anxiety/struggled, and notice how by just eliminating the emotions part of it, its just another story than an experience.

Please read out loud what is following now:

'AS IT IS'.

You must be wondering what is this, and why so much of emphasis on this three word statement. The reason I am stressing so much on this is simply because this one statement helped me change my life and taught me to be at peace with absolutely everything. Whenever I am faced with a situation where things may not seem to be in my favour, I remind myself to look at the situation 'as it is' without attaching my emotions or my intelligence on how it should be for me to be comfortable with it. And the moment I do that, the complete resistance from my end to deal with that particular situation just disappears, and I am eventually lead to see the positive in what's happening. As I continue to do so, I eventually get results in my favour. But the best part is it doesn't even bother me then whatever the result may be.

CHAPTER 12

Insights Around
Unspoken Agreements

"If you talk to a man in a language he understands, that goes to his head. If you talk to him in his language, that goes to his heart"

– Nelson Mandela

The origin of unspoken agreement lies in the language. Language plays an important role in creating impressions on our thinking; we have seen the importance of thoughts in the previous chapters in designing our life. We should be careful of what we speak as we are listening to those words.

For example: If I continuously keep saying that its very difficult for me to forgive or to lose weight then irrespective of my efforts these targets will be very difficult for me to accomplish. We also have understood how subconscious keeps up all the information from around us but we don't know that its also absorbing the information coming from us. There is no filter in our brain and it doesn't even judge what is good for us and what's not, so when we are dealing with such a obedient wish fulfilling organ it becomes more than important to use the right kind of words even for ourselves.

That means if we are continuously using critical words or abusive talk then our thoughts also become critical and we would end up attracting more situations in life where we would demonstrate this behavior as LIKE ATTRACTS LIKE. So mindfully lets use words which would bring us peace and not stress.

By using same words in all life situations we may end up creating a "**life theme**" which would resonate with those words

For instance: If somebody keeps saying that that "Its not fair" faced in any kind of situation then the possibility of that person creating a life where there would always be a question of fairness would be very high.

Now once we have understood the importance language has, lets use it for our advantage, to help us achieve our goals, by picking right kind of words. A simple example of that would be if you want to be rich, don't use words like "*I want to be rich*" because here you are focusing on the wantingness; you will end up feeling the want more and more than actually reaching anywhere. So rather than that use words like, "*I am getting richer day by day*" hence changing the emotion from deprivation to abundance.

Another paradigm of communication is a Self-talk or popularly known as <u>Internal Dialogue</u>., Irrespective of whether we notice or not internal dialogue does play a very important role in our dealings with the external world, as most of these words of our dialogue are based out of perceptions created by us through observation of other people like our parents, friends, family, or also of our surroundings. For instance if we have grown up with a critical parent/s then the probability of we using critical language with ourselves is comparatively high. That may also reflect in our thinking as well as in our communication with others as well and in our outlook towards life.

Hence, it's crucial to choose positive words when you are talking to yourself. We tend to be angry or cynic and judgmental as well, and that's what reflects in our conversations and our attitude toward others. This kind of attitude blocks our true feelings from flowing, as humans our true essence is love and peace, and being judgmental comes from a space of fear; hence, depriving us from an opportunity to be our true self.

There have been studies, which say that not just words, even alphabets—the sound they create seems to have an impact on our brain and our collective thinking. For example, if we start saying 'OM', without even knowing the meaning of it, still—for reasons unknown by us—we will feel good and peaceful from within as, it is of frequency of 7.83Hz, which also happens to be Mother Earth's natural heartbeat rhythm, also known as Schumann Resonance.

Sometimes, to make the words more impactful, we can also use our breath, like by focusing on breath if you say positive affirmations daily, your brain will do respond to them in your favor. Along with breath our body poses can also benefit us in a lot of ways. Like if you are getting ready for an interview, sitting with your spine straight or using a 'superman pose' can help you induce a new level of confidence from within.

Words are very important, as per the book *Words Can Change Your Brain* by Dr Andrew Newberg, a neuroscientist at Thomas Jefferson University, and Mark Robert Waldman, a communications expert, *'A single word has the power to influence the expression of genes that regulate physical and emotional stress.'* The experts, as per the book, believe that using right kind of words can change your reality.

> *By holding a positive and optimistic word in your mind, you stimulate frontal lobe activity. This area includes specific language centres that connect directly to the motor cortex responsible for moving you into action. And as our research has shown, the longer you concentrate on positive words, the more you begin to affect other areas of the brain. Functions in the parietal lobe start to change, which changes your perception of yourself and the people you interact with. A positive view of yourself will bias you toward seeing the good in others, whereas a negative self-image will include you toward suspicion and doubt. Over time, the structure of your thalamus will also change in response to your conscious words, thoughts, and feelings, and we believe*

> *that the thalamic changes affect the way in*
> *which you perceive reality.'*

So lets consciously use proper words and create the right kind of agreements with ourself.

The concept of heaven and hell post death is really questionable. We have been given this as a bait in order for us to behave in a certain manner. But nobody cares, as most of us think, 'Okay, so after death, I will pay for my sins. As long as I am here, let me live the way I want.' But the truth is we are right now creating heaven or hell wherever we are with our words, our thoughts, and our emotions; and not just for others, but also for ourselves. Collectively, if we continue living in fear, hatred, anger, we will manage to create a world so toxic that no hope or love could survive; and we are doing it for our families, our loved ones, and ourselves.

Most of the chronic illnesses occur due to dysfunction of our immune system, which can be directly influenced by the feeling of rejection or loneliness, also by being irritable and angry. We need to ask ourselves why are we doing this and who is going to benefit from it.

As seen in one of the previous chapter in a relationship, we need to stop asking 'what about me?' As we do that, the whole essence of love is lost as this question emerges from our deep-seated fears and insecurity along with space of neediness. We all need to choose a more love-based existence. As history has it, whenever fear has become the main core of existence, it has lead to extinction, and we cannot change the world without changing the world within. Each one of us plays a pivotal role in creating the change much desired, so let's shoulder the responsibility and start from this moment by forgiving and start empathizing than questioning and criticizing. Love is not expendable or limited. More you give, more you will receive, and will have more to give. Let's be the source.

In order to be a good communicator there are a few things, which can be kept in mind like by placing the emphasis on the right kind of words you, can change the meaning of a sentence; look at the phrase "**I need happiness in my life**". With stress on every word, the meaning of the sentence changes significantly.

"**I** need happiness in my life"
"I **need** happiness in my life"
"I need **happiness** in my life"
"I need happiness **in** my life"
"I need happiness in **my** life"
"I need happiness in my **life**"

When one person is talking in the communication, he/she is just one part of that interaction. The other part is happening in the head of the listener. Depending on listener's mood, belief, energy level, the meaning he/she draws is independent of the person who is talking. So the unspoken agreement is fragile. The breach of it is even more fragile, as when in any situation when there is another person involved, you have no control whatsoever on their response. Especially with unspoken agreement as it mostly originates in your own head. Having said that when we are actually communicating with somebody it's important to have an open mind and to be patient, leaving our assumptions aside, as the meaning of communication is the response it evokes.

As we continue to understand about unspoken agreements we realize what they are, how they are created, and how we can change them to experience healthy and fulfilling relationships. Along with that we also saw the importance of monitoring your thoughts and usage of right kind of language can actually help us create the kind of life we desire, because here we are taking the control and responsibility for our self than giving away our power to every situation or a person coming in our life. The most important thing to have a great relationship with others is to first learn to have a wonderful relationship with I/me/myself. So let's together take this first step in creating a wonderful relationship with our self by creating some Spoken Agreements with our own self. Let's promise our own self to respect and honor each of these agreements, as they will lead us to being happy and free. Here lets take the charge of our life and the first step towards doing it is by making our own Spoken Agreements.

Some of the spoken agreements that I have found immensely valuable are listed below. Please feel free to create more and add them to this list. Make your own list.

- ❖ I will love and approve of myself completely.
- ❖ I will focus on winning people than winning an argument.
- ❖ I will let go off the need of being right.
- ❖ I would treat others the way I would treat myself, and before I do that, I would treat myself with lot of love and acceptance.

❖ I would focus on the issue rather than having an issue with the person.

❖ I would be assertive and soft-spoken at the same time.

❖ I would live life to the fullest.

❖ I would always give my 100 per cent and stay detached with the results.

❖ I will use my words to heal and not hurt.

❖ I will use humor to cut through the seriousness of life.

❖ In relationship, I will act from space of unconditional love and not from space of fear or insecurity.

Let the above list be as long as you want, make as many agreements as you wish as each of these agreements are your command to yourself for being ultimately joyful and live your life to its fullest.

There are a few sheets at the end of the book for you to jot down your Spoken Agreements.

Learning to live, by learning to Love.

Everything we do in life is mainly to feel loved. Our most basic and true need is to feel loved. No matter what work we do, it gives us some sense of feeling good about ourselves (i.e. self-love). We crave every success or accomplishment, because it allows us to love ourselves. Even the need to accumulate materialistic things, enhancing our lifestyle and entertaining our senses eventually provides us with some kind of feeling good about ourselves. The only caveat in this is that if any of these things are taken away from us, our feeling good about ourselves also starts to diminish. We start loathing or hating and getting frustrated with ourselves.

Here, I want to share a small hypothesis about how our experience of life may have started. Imagine you were living in this heavenly place with all the possible beauty of nature. You are absolutely happy and eventually 'being in bliss' has become your ethos. All the thoughts and feelings are just about harmony and peace and nothing else. You are enveloped with love like a halo around you, providing you the warmth and lightness inside, as well as outside. Then one day, deep in the forest, as you are busy appreciating the flowers, for some reason you lose your way to your abode of heaven. You notice this and suddenly a worry creeps in. Now, somehow, that halo also does not seem to be around your thoughts also are kind of conflicting with your nature of being in bliss, you are not comfortable being in this state. Then suddenly, you see a butterfly, and you think to yourself that you have noticed this butterfly earlier as well, and feel like you should follow it. As you surrender your worry and start following the butterfly, before you know it you are back to your abode of heaven. Everything is just the way it was. You get your halo back, and now for some reason, this remembrance – feeling of lost and found again - seem to magnify your 'feeling of bliss'. You are more ecstatic than before, and you simply love this experience of knowing/ experiencing, then forgetting and remembering again. So you decide I want to make this more fun than it was, so you choose your life situations, experiences, people, even their behaviour—almost everything you feel will give you the best feeling of remembrance. And once you are ready with this plot, you command your mind to forget everything about your true self.

But the mind is resistant to the idea of losing it completely. So you assure the mind that the butterfly, to whom you have to surrender and follow, will always be there. You simply need to notice and follow to get you back to where you originally belong. So nothing to worry and with this assurance, the mind agrees. This is probably when you decide to take birth and start your experience of remembering. Needless to say who the butterfly is... (The first answer your mind has given, yeah, that's right).

Now with this story as a reference, think of all those people in your life who rejected you or disappointed you or did not love you the way you wanted. Understand and thank these people, as they have played their individual role in bringing you close to your true nature. They provided you with an opportunity to stop looking for love outside and realize that it was always inside of you. You are full of love so release all these people of your complaints, resentments, and regrets. Bless them as much as possible. They have done what they were supposed to do. Be grateful for those who have genuinely loved you; thus, giving you a live demonstration of how you can love yourself. Know this fact that you cannot give something unless you have it, so if you have people you truly love its because there is a vast reservoir of love within you already, its just a matter of how you choose to access it and for whom.

With all the understanding and experience I have regarding Life, I feel these are some simple truths about life:

1. We all are one.
2. We are not supposed to go anywhere or reach anywhere.
3. Life is meaningless; it has all the meaning we give it.
4. All the life experiences are happening inside of us.
5. We are more than just this body or mind.
6. All our fears are self-created.
7. No event or experience has power to define us.
8. To reach somewhere you have to start moving from where you are
9. Change is inevitable
10. All healing is Self-healing
11. Give to Get, and also Get to be able to Give
12. Having gratitude is the right attitude
13. If no peace within there is no point of anything
14. Treat your body with respect
15. Every moment arriving in our life is full of grace
16. Reflect and Project
17. True success is in being humble
18. If you don't know how to forgive you will never know how to be human
19. Being one with Nature can help us capture our true essence
20. Love and acceptance can make us more receptive of life.
21. Don't write-off anything or anybody

CHAPTER 13

Below is a story that can help us derive inspiration on how to live a full life and be satisfied with what we have.

Maya

I got out from the bed dreading if it's already a Monday morning. As I forced myself out of the bed, I felt a severe head rush along with all the things from previous night that just rushed back at me. I rubbed my forehead in a false attempt to make my headache go away. Slowly heading towards the bathroom, I stumble on a heart-shaped pillow. Somehow balancing myself, giving it an irritated glare, as I can't help but notice the big smile drawn on it with three bold letters written 'I LOVE YOU'. My thoughts just pause, as I am trying to feel something when I see them, as there was a time when these words and that pillow meant so much to me. Well, I remind myself of the time, and how late I was getting for work.

I gather myself together and hold my toothbrush, wondering about the paste. My eyes go towards the mirror, and I see my face. Disappointingly, all I can notice is the sadness and ugliness it has all over it, the tiny pigmentation, the eyebrows that needs reshaping, and the pale colour of my skin, which could have easily switched places with the dark circles under my eyes. 'Well,' I say to myself, and finally succeed in locating the toothpaste.

As I swiftly finish my other chores after half an hour, I am out of the door still trying to understand whether this half an hour was the longest or the most hurried time of my life. As I get out of the building and start toward the direction of my office, I am wondering what's wrong. I have always had challenges and have learnt my way of getting through it, then what is it today that my entire past seems to be flashing in front of me? Why am I feeling so low? Am I dying? Is this what it feels like to be at a low point? As I am lost in these thoughts, a beautiful woman passes across me. I can't help but notice how perfect her figure is and what a beautiful branded dress she is wearing. I say to myself, 'Only if,' while letting out a big sigh. As I do this, I feel like something is coming back to me. I can't place it exactly, but it feels like this has happened before. And then I chuckle to myself saying that this happens every time I see any woman other than me and remind myself of my inadequacy.

Suddenly, a cab pulls right next to me, and the driver wants to know where I need to go. I think, without my knowledge, I may have called for the cab. I tell him the address and get inside. As the cab starts, I start noticing the tall buildings and see all the people busy trying to reach somewhere. My eyes desperately are trying to look for somebody's smile or even the best a baby's smile, but hard luck, I reach office where everybody almost have the same expression on their faces. I think of what's happening. Am I in a mid-life crisis situation? Maybe I need to see a shrink? But I am not feeling hopeless or suicidal. All I want to see and feel is some hope. Then why is this happening? I really wish somebody could answer these questions for me.

I reach my desk and see the files piled and the mess created by all the papers just lying around. As I am straightening out the mess, I stop and look around me; and for that moment, I am not able to hear anything. Even the people around me are blurring, everything around me just ceases to exist, and I see myself standing in this pitch-dark space. I feel scared, as there is nowhere to go. I want to yell, but am sure that nobody will hear me, so I just become still and start noticing my thoughts as I go back to the party I attended last night where I met this woman who had so much of glow on her face, though she didn't have perfect skin, but that nowhere made her look any less beautiful than she was. All the people in the party either felt attracted by her exuberance or felt threatened, but yeah, there was nobody in the party who didn't notice her.

She was just smiling, shaking hands, and genuinely connecting with people. I asked the woman standing next to me, 'Who is she?' She said her name is Maya. She is a teacher in high school. She also teaches and practises yoga. Still, my curiosity was not pacified and stood there wanting to know more about her. Understanding my eagerness, she continued and told me that Maya was an orphan, and after making her way through a lot of foster homes, she finally ran away from the last home she was adopted in and came to New York. She struggled for food and shelter here. Also at worst days, resorted to prostitution, but finally managed to get herself a job at café where she could at least take care of her basic needs; with that, she also pursued her education and ended up doing well for herself. In fact, last year, she also got engaged; but unfortunately, her fiancé broke off the engagement when he learnt that she had last stage breast cancer, and her chances of survival were pretty slick. Post that, she quit her job at this big multinational and volunteers at homes, spending time with poor and needy and helping them in every way possible.

As I heard this, I kept on waiting for this woman to say more and talk about some happy ending about Maya, but she didn't say anything after that. I got shocked that what's wrong with Maya, then what is she so happy about? I have to know it. Maybe this woman does not know her entire story.

I spoke to more couple of people about Maya, a little here and there but the outline of the story was same. Finally, I couldn't hold on to my curiosity, and I landed in front of Maya. With this confused look on my face, I said, 'Please tell me what's your secret of life, and put me out of my misery as I fail to understand how even after such a difficult life, you are so peaceful and happy. What did u do to change your life?

She smiled and said, 'I HAPPENED TO LIFE AND BECAME ONE WITH it.'

I kept staring at her, trying to figure out its meaning. Somehow, I felt like something had hit me right on my head. Then all I can remember is that I had lots to drink and was dropped home by a colleague. And now in this room, the meaning of Maya's words are coming to me. (Don't postpone life/happiness, start being happy right in this moment where you are, starting from the fact that you are breathing without you doing anything to make it happen. Which means you are alive. And understand "don't add days to life but add life to days." That means that even if there is something you are not happy with in your life, you still have an opportunity to change it and make your life better. So open your eyes and see what's real. Don't hide behind false layers. Let your real self shine through. Make the most of what you got, as life is in this moment right here, right now.)

As I manage to get back to my senses, I feel like I was levitating and thrown right back on ground. But as I regained my awareness in every sense, everything has started to seem beautiful; and all of a sudden, I feel this gratitude toward life and so many of its offerings, which I had taken for granted. And right now, in this moment, I make this spoken agreement with myself that I will not just live life to its fullest, but also enrich the lives of as many people around me.

'Be a light unto yourself. Be a lamp unto yourself.'
Don't search for light anywhere else; the light is already
there, the fire is already there. Just probe a little deeper
into your being. Inquire. Maybe much ash has gathered
around the fire. Just probe deep inside, and you will find
the spark again. And once you have found a single spark
inside yourself, you will become a flame soon. You will be a
fire, a fire that purifies, a fire that transforms, a fire that
gives you a new birth and a new being.'

— Last Words of Buddha

Self-Intervention:

1. What is . . . supposed to do?
   (Write the name of the person in the blanks) and answer
   the question.

   ....

2. What am/was I supposed to do?
   (Make a note of what you think your action could be/
   have been) and write it below.

   ....

3. Name the emotion you are feeling right now.
   (It could be one or more than one, list all of them)

   ....

4. Are you open to the idea to feel an emotion more
   comfortable/peaceful
   (Answer you could be both yes/no, but if the answer is
   no, then it means you are still unwilling to forgive the
   other person, then I would suggest pick another person
   for now and again start with question1)

   ....

5. What could probably be the UA?
(State in your words what possibly is the UA you are dealing with here, and if you could also try and guess what the other person's UA could have been, by doing this we can get a quick resolution)

....

6. Now say this power statement to yourself: 'I am releasing myself and the other person* of this UA"(state the UA)*(Name of the person)
(Say it out loud and as you are saying it notice the emotion within, and if the emotion is still negative then we have to keep saying it till the time we don't change it to a positive/neutral emotion, if you face difficulties in doing so first think of a Higher power* and ask for help and second use the process where we stress on one word and say the above statement, to understand how to do this better check out last chapter of the book, also make a note that first time when you say you may state the UA but if you need to repeat then just say the power statement, your brain is smart enough to know what you are doing and will help you with the same)
*Higher power could be anything from the God you believe to nature or your values, anything which you regard to be superior

....

7. Terminate the unspoken agreement by writing this on a piece of paper, then either throw it away or dispose in a way which would give you a feeling of release.

....

8. Make a note of your emotion.

....

9. Create a new agreement with yourself, which would make you feel liberated rather than bounded. (Write the new agreement)

....

10. Declare it.(If possible tell somebody about it, like your best friend/spouse/anybody whom you feel like)

....

Self-Intervention:

1. What is . . . supposed to do?
   (Write the name of the person in the blanks) and answer the question.

   ....

2. What am/was I supposed to do?
   (Make a note of what you think your action could be/have been) and write it below.

   ....

3. Name the emotion you are feeling right now.
   (It could be one or more than one, list all of them)

   ....

4. Are you open to the idea to feel an emotion more comfortable/peaceful
   (Answer you could be both yes/no, but if the answer is no, then it means you are still unwilling to forgive the other person, then I would suggest pick another person for now and again start with question1)

   ....

5. What could probably be the UA?
    (State in your words what possibly is the UA you are
    dealing with here, and if you could also try and guess
    what the other person's UA could have been, by doing
    this we can get a quick resolution)

    ....

6. Now say this power statement to yourself: 'I am
    releasing myself and the other person* of this UA"(state
    the UA)*(Name of the person)
    (Say it out loud and as you are saying it notice the
    emotion within, and if the emotion is still negative then
    we have to keep saying it till the time we don't change
    it to a positive/neutral emotion, if you face difficulties
    in doing so first think of a Higher power* and ask for
    help and second use the process where we stress on one
    word and say the above statement, to understand how
    to do this better check out last chapter of the book, also
    make a note that first time when you say you may state
    the UA but if you need to repeat then just say the power
    statement, your brain is smart enough to know what you
    are doing and will help you with the same)
    *Higher power could be anything from the God you
    believe to nature or your values, anything which you
    regard to be superior

    ....

7. Terminate the unspoken agreement by writing this on a piece of paper, then either throw it away or dispose in a way which would give you a feeling of release.

   ....

8. Make a note of your emotion.

   ....

9. Create a new agreement with yourself, which would make you feel liberated rather than bounded.
   (Write the new agreement)

   ....

10. Declare it.(If possible tell somebody about it, like your best friend/spouse/anybody whom you feel like)

    ....

Self-Intervention:

1. What is . . . supposed to do?
    (Write the name of the person in the blanks) and answer
    the question.

    ....

2. What am/was I supposed to do?
    (Make a note of what you think your action could be/
    have been) and write it below.

    ....

3. Name the emotion you are feeling right now.
    (It could be one or more than one, list all of them)

    ....

4. Are you open to the idea to feel an emotion more
    comfortable/peaceful
    (Answer you could be both yes/no, but if the answer is
    no, then it means you are still unwilling to forgive the
    other person, then I would suggest pick another person
    for now and again start with question1)

    ....

5. What could probably be the UA?
   (State in your words what possibly is the UA you are dealing with here, and if you could also try and guess what the other person's UA could have been, by doing this we can get a quick resolution)

   ....

6. Now say this power statement to yourself: 'I am releasing myself and the other person* of this UA"(state the UA)*(Name of the person)
   (Say it out loud and as you are saying it notice the emotion within, and if the emotion is still negative then we have to keep saying it till the time we don't change it to a positive/neutral emotion, if you face difficulties in doing so first think of a Higher power* and ask for help and second use the process where we stress on one word and say the above statement, to understand how to do this better check out last chapter of the book, also make a note that first time when you say you may state the UA but if you need to repeat then just say the power statement, your brain is smart enough to know what you are doing and will help you with the same)
   *Higher power could be anything from the God you believe to nature or your values, anything which you regard to be superior

   ....

7. Terminate the unspoken agreement by writing this on a piece of paper, then either throw it away or dispose in a way which would give you a feeling of release.

....

8. Make a note of your emotion.

....

9. Create a new agreement with yourself, which would make you feel liberated rather than bounded.
   (Write the new agreement)

....

10. Declare it.(If possible tell somebody about it, like your best friend/spouse/anybody whom you feel like)

....

Self-Intervention:

1. What is . . . supposed to do?
   (Write the name of the person in the blanks) and answer
   the question.

   ....

2. What am/was I supposed to do?
   (Make a note of what you think your action could be/
   have been) and write it below.

   ....

3. Name the emotion you are feeling right now.
   (It could be one or more than one, list all of them)

   ....

4. Are you open to the idea to feel an emotion more
   comfortable/peaceful
   (Answer you could be both yes/no, but if the answer is
   no, then it means you are still unwilling to forgive the
   other person, then I would suggest pick another person
   for now and again start with question1)

   ....

5. What could probably be the UA?
   (State in your words what possibly is the UA you are dealing with here, and if you could also try and guess what the other person's UA could have been, by doing this we can get a quick resolution)

   ....

6. Now say this power statement to yourself: 'I am releasing myself and the other person* of this UA"(state the UA)*(Name of the person)
   (Say it out loud and as you are saying it notice the emotion within, and if the emotion is still negative then we have to keep saying it till the time we don't change it to a positive/neutral emotion, if you face difficulties in doing so first think of a Higher power* and ask for help and second use the process where we stress on one word and say the above statement, to understand how to do this better check out last chapter of the book, also make a note that first time when you say you may state the UA but if you need to repeat then just say the power statement, your brain is smart enough to know what you are doing and will help you with the same)
   *Higher power could be anything from the God you believe to nature or your values, anything which you regard to be superior

   ....

7. Terminate the unspoken agreement by writing this on a piece of paper, then either throw it away or dispose in a way which would give you a feeling of release.

    ....

8. Make a note of your emotion.

    ....

9. Create a new agreement with yourself, which would make you feel liberated rather than bounded.
   (Write the new agreement)

    ....

10. Declare it.(If possible tell somebody about it, like your best friend/spouse/anybody whom you feel like)

    ....

Self-Intervention:

1. What is . . . supposed to do?
   (Write the name of the person in the blanks) and answer
   the question.

   ....

2. What am/was I supposed to do?
   (Make a note of what you think your action could be/
   have been) and write it below.

   ....

3. Name the emotion you are feeling right now.
   (It could be one or more than one, list all of them)

   ....

4. Are you open to the idea to feel an emotion more
   comfortable/peaceful
   (Answer you could be both yes/no, but if the answer is
   no, then it means you are still unwilling to forgive the
   other person, then I would suggest pick another person
   for now and again start with question1)

   ....

5. What could probably be the UA?
    (State in your words what possibly is the UA you are dealing with here, and if you could also try and guess what the other person's UA could have been, by doing this we can get a quick resolution)

    ....

6. Now say this power statement to yourself: 'I am releasing myself and the other person* of this UA"(state the UA)*(Name of the person)
    (Say it out loud and as you are saying it notice the emotion within, and if the emotion is still negative then we have to keep saying it till the time we don't change it to a positive/neutral emotion, if you face difficulties in doing so first think of a Higher power* and ask for help and second use the process where we stress on one word and say the above statement, to understand how to do this better check out last chapter of the book, also make a note that first time when you say you may state the UA but if you need to repeat then just say the power statement, your brain is smart enough to know what you are doing and will help you with the same)
    *Higher power could be anything from the God you believe to nature or your values, anything which you regard to be superior

    ....

7. Terminate the unspoken agreement by writing this on a piece of paper, then either throw it away or dispose in a way which would give you a feeling of release.

....

8. Make a note of your emotion.

....

9. Create a new agreement with yourself, which would make you feel liberated rather than bounded.
   (Write the new agreement)

....

10. Declare it.(If possible tell somebody about it, like your best friend/spouse/anybody whom you feel like)

....

SPOKEN AGREEMENTS

....

....

....

....

....

....

....

....

....

....

SPOKEN AGREEMENTS

....

....

....

....

....

....

....

....

....

....

Printed in the United States
By Bookmasters